FREE TO OBEY

Johann Chapoutot

FREE TO OBEY

HOW THE NAZIS INVENTED
MODERN MANAGEMENT

*Translated from the French
by Steven Rendall*

Europa
editions

Europa Editions
27 Union Square West, Suite 302
New York NY 10003
www.europaeditions.com
info@europaeditons.com

Copyright © Editions Gallimard, Paris, 2020
First English publication 2023 by Europa Editions

Translation by Steven Rendall
Original title: *Libres d'obéir*
Translation copyright © 2023 by Europa Editions

Library of Congress Cataloging in Publication Data is available
ISBN 978-1-60945-804-1

Chapoutot, Johann
Free to Obey

Book design by Emanuele Ragnisco
www.mekkanografici.com

Cover image: Shawshots /Alamy Stock Photo

Prepress by Grafica Punto Print – Rome

Printed in the USA

CONTENTS

To Hortense Chapoutot
Because, like a rainbow, she comes in colors

FREE TO OBEY

To us, they seem stubbornly foreign and yet strangely close, almost our contemporaries. "They" are the Nazi criminals whose lives and acts historians of this period observe by reading their writings, as well as reconstructing their mental universe and careers.

They are absolutely foreign in their ideas and in their life experiences. We are not thuggish mercenaries like Dirlewanger[1] or Krüger,[2] veterans of the trenches who became professional killers and terrorists. We are not passionately devoted to violence and control, to teaching others to kill, like Heydrich[3] or Himmler. Their brutality and fanaticism, as well as their mediocrity, make them as distant from us as the black-and-white images and the cut of their uniforms suggest.

This also holds true for Herbert Backe.[4] Backe was a man of another time and another place, rendered opaque and remote by his exotic background and by a life that none of us knows or can imagine. He was born in the Empire of the Czars in 1896, because his father, a merchant, was engaged in business there. He studied at the secondary school in Tiflis, the capital of Georgia, where the young Stalin also lived. Between 1914 and 1918, he was imprisoned as a German citizen; after his release, he went to Germany, where he studied agronomy. A self-proclaimed expert on Russia, which he purported to know well, he became a convinced racist, certain that Germans were biologically and culturally superior. In his view, they were destined to dominate the vast, fertile lands of Eastern Europe. A member of the Nazi party and a farmer, he pursued a political career. While a unit leader and representative in the Prussian assembly, he also turned his mind to theory. In his 1931 brochure entitled *German Peasant, Awaken!* he advocated the colonization of Eastern Europe and naturally scorned the local populations, which he saw as mere auxiliaries, at best, of German prosperity.

Behind his round glasses and delicate features, Backe was a violent radical. That pleased Himmler, the head of the SS, and his agricultural specialist, Richard Darré, under whom Backe worked as a state secretary in the Ministry of Agriculture before replacing him as *de facto* minister in 1942. In the meantime, from 1936 on, he became an agricultural expert for the administration of the Four Year Plan directed by Hermann Goering. In 1941, he provided Goering with the inspiration for a policy of systematic starvation in the Eastern territories that the Reich was preparing to conquer and colonize. This "Hunger Plan" was intended to feed the Reich by expropriating the Soviet people's food supply, and Backe coolly acknowledged that, in the medium term, it would likely cause the death of thirty million people, a result he considered desirable. He was such a dyed-in-the-wool Nazi that, while imprisoned in Nuremberg, Backe was still moved by the words of encouragement and congratulation that had been showered on him by Hitler. As a minister, a general in the SS, and the main planner entrusted with supplying food to the East, Backe had had a brilliant career under the Third Reich, whose collapse he could not accept. In 1947, he committed suicide in his prison cell, exactly forty years after his father took his own life.

Such a career, such ideas, and such a personality are absolutely alien to us. Even a historian familiar with Nazis and their writings, seeking to understand how human beings could come to think and act in this way, cannot—when looking up from the documents, when putting down reading glasses to give the subject some distance—avoid the nausea and horror provoked by the words and portraits of this slender little man, the fervent ideologue, the conscientious technician.

Exploring the life and universe of these people takes one through foreign, distant lands steeped in fear and brutality, and past times that came to an absolute end, we think, in 1945.

However, as we peruse them, there are moments when, on reading a word or a phrase, the past suddenly appears to be present. I experienced this feeling a few years ago when I was reading and commenting on one of Backe's texts whose trenchant brevity makes it all the more violent. On the eve of the attack on the USSR, in preparation for the conquest and colonization of the East, Backe, who was then the state secretary in the Reich Food Supply and Agriculture Ministry, wrote a three-page handbook organized in twelve points, a list of instructions intended for the German administrators of the Four Year Plan and of his ministry who were to implement the plan in the East.[5] We have already noted the foreignness of this text: its racism with regard to Russians, who are seen as "dialecticians," liars, fanatics, and backward; its exaltation of the German "lord and master" (*Herrenmensch*) as compared with the Soviet subhuman (*Untermensch*); its colonialist brutality, which stinks of the whip and the concentration camp. But other parts of this text are familiar to us, things that we seem to have heard or read elsewhere, in other contexts. Herbert Backe demands "performance" from his agents: "What matters is to act," to "make decisions rapidly," "without worrying about bureaucratic scruples (*keine Aktenwirtschaft*)." "Don't talk, act," without "whining or complaining about supervision (*nach oben*)." Supervisors establish an "objective" (*Endziel*) that the agents are expected to achieve as soon as possible, without asking for additional means, without moaning or relenting when faced with the difficulty of the task. What is important is that the mission be accomplished, no matter how. Backe recommends "the greatest elasticity in the methods" employed. These "methods are left to the discretion of each individual." Since the nineteenth century, this conception of the job has a name in military terminology: *Auftragstaktik*, mission-type tactics or objective tactics. An assignment is given to an officer, who must carry it out as he sees fit and as he can, so long as the objective is realized.

"Elasticity" (we would call it "flexibility," "initiative," or "agility"), "achievement," "objective," "mission"—here we find ourselves on familiar ground. The dinosaur Backe, that archaic, distant monster wearing an SS uniform, rejoins our time and place, because he uses its words and categories, thinks in its terms and lives its ideas. He sees himself and experiences himself as an "achiever" (*Leistungsmensch*) and regrets that his protector and superior Darré, who he views as too spineless, is a "loser" (*Versager*).[6]

Backe was convinced that life was a battle in which only strong-willed and high-achieving people prevailed: in short, a zero-sum game in which the "losers" paid a high price for their inferiority and their failures. He was, like all his co-workers and comrades in the party, a Social Darwinist who thought of the world as an arena. Since resources are limited, individuals—and, according to his racist perspective, species—are engaged in a life-or-death struggle to gain access to those resources and to control them. As an agronomist, Backe, whose name suggests, in German, the verb "bake" (*backen*), thought in terms of territories to be conquered and food to be supplied. These obsessions were very understandable for a German whose country had experienced famine during World War I, but they are very remote for those of us who are used to having access to everything, in abundance, on the shelves of our supermarkets—unless the collapse of climatic systems puts that question back on the agenda. Backe had Nazi obsessions and ideas, but he spoke a language that is also used by our world, its social organization and its economy.

Herbert Backe's responsibilities and high offices led him

to take an interest in the organization of labor and leadership (*Menschenführung*)—what we call "management." He was not the only one; far from it. As we shall see, some Nazis even made this a career and a life's work after the war. There is certainly nothing astonishing about it. Germany constructed a complex, developed economy with a powerful and highly productive industry in which consulting engineers sought to find the optimal organization of the work force—as they did in France, the United States, the United Kingdom and elsewhere in Europe. Management has a history that began long before Nazism, but this history was researched and reflected on during the twelve years of the Third Reich, a managerial phase that became the mold for the theory and practice of management in the postwar period.

The recognition after 1945 that the mass atrocity crimes had been an *industry* elicited harsh, bitter reflections on capitalist organization and on our modernity. The wise sociologist and thinker Zygmunt Bauman left his mark by publishing *Modernity and the Holocaust*, showing that the absolute horror of the Nazis' crimes was perhaps less archaic than contemporary: a certain economic and social organization, and an impressive mastery of logistics, made possible, or even promoted, a series of crimes that were casually attributed to the most backward barbarism rather than to the disciplined structure of a resolutely modern enterprise. The thought of people like Bauman—or like the philosopher Giorgio Agamben, who sees in the *camp* the paradigmatic site of social control, of the hierarchization and reification characteristic of our modernity—has certainly helped remove restraints on historians, who feel increasingly free to study the contemporaneity of Nazism, the way in which this phenomenon came to mark our time and its tendencies, and was revealed to be their sign or symptom. Thus, the crimes against humanity were understood by authors like Götz Aly[7] as the expression of rational political and economic projects decided upon by technocrats and *managers* (the word is increasingly common among historians of the period) who moved groups of people around, starved territories, and advocated the exploitation of people's vital energies to the point of completely exhausting them—and did so with a completely remarkable professional detachment and coolness (Himmler called it "decency").

Some detailed studies have been devoted to these managers, such as Oswald Pohl, the head of the SS's Main Economic and Administrative Office;[8] Hans Kammler,[9] head of the same office's "Construction" Department, who was responsible, after 1943, for ensuring the security of strategic products in the concentration camp empire (in this capacity, he set up the V2 factory at the Mittelbau-Dora camp); and Albert Speer, who has recently been the subject of numerous biographies.[10] Speer now interests us less as an architect or indulgent witness than as the man who, starting in 1942, was the great organizer of the war economy, the modernist technician, the capable administrator—in short, the supreme manager of the Reich's industries.

In light of these works, it has become possible to see that there was something criminal in the very notion of the management and "administration" of "human resources," as the film *La Question humaine* (2007; English title *Heartbeat Detector*) suggested emphatically and skillfully. There is a certain logic in the passage from the objectification of human beings, seen as "material," "resources," or "production factors," to their use and even destruction, a logic whose paradigmatic site is the concentration camp, where, from 1939 on, people were forced to engage in economic production and worked to death.

All this could be developed and discussed at length, but that is not my purpose here. Nor do I seek to present an indictment of managers, management, human resources departments, or auditors of consulting firms. Some of the people in this field are atrocious, but many have embraced this career for humanitarian reasons and do their best to reduce the work-related suffering of the employees they direct or advise. A few of them have even become remarkable sociologists of labor.[11]

Put more simply, in a time when management occupies people's minds as much as the question of salvation used to, when "personnel departments" have become "HR" (to manage human "resources"),[12] we have to adopt a broader, more distanced view: why, in what context, and in response to what needs, did the Nazis reflect on the organization of labor, on the distribution of tasks, and on the structure of institutions in public administration and the private economy? What conception of management did they develop? In their reflections, what became of labor, the individual, civil service, and the state?

These questions are interesting in themselves, because they bolster the claim that Nazism is a modern phenomenon belonging to our time and place—the contemporary world. They become even more interesting if we note that the Nazi conception of management continued after 1945, through the height of Germany's "economic miracle," and that former senior officials in the SS were not only its theorists but also its successful practitioners, achieving a reconstruction as spectacular as it was remunerative.

My point is neither essentialist nor genealogical: I do not claim that management has Nazi origins (the former precedes the latter by several decades), nor do I claim that it is an activity that is criminal by nature.

I am simply proposing a case study based on two observations that pertain to the world in which we live and work: the young lawyers, academics, and high officials of the Third Reich thought a great deal about managerial questions, because the Nazi enterprise had gargantuan requirements in terms of the mobilization of resources and the organization of labor. Paradoxically, it promoted a non-authoritarian conception of labor, in which the employee and the worker accepted their fate and approved of their activities, in a realm of freedom and autonomy that was, in theory, very incompatible with the illiberal character of the Third Reich. This form of labor "through joy" (*durch Freude*) prospered after 1945 and is familiar to us today, at a time when "commitment," "motivation," and "involvement" are supposed to proceed from the "pleasure" of working and from organized "benevolence."

Those who did the work were granted autonomy in the methods they chose, so despite being unable to define or set the objectives, they found themselves all the more responsible—and, in this case, guilty—if the mission failed.

But let's not get ahead of ourselves. Let's proceed step by step to see how jurists and administrators think and act. The first question we need to ask is this: how does one manage an ever-expanding Reich with fewer workers and resources to support it?

CHAPTER 1
CONCEIVING THE ADMINISTRATION OF THE GREAT REICH

The time was "historic." Nazi discourse was fond of hyperbole and bragging. Judging by the texts, speeches, pictures, and films, everything was "historic," "unique" (*einmalig*), "gigantic," "decisive" (*entscheidend*), and so on, *ad nauseam*. This was arguably the case for a certain category of activists, agents, and (senior) officials. These military, administrative, and political managers of the government of "national recovery" were enthusiastic, because careers, benefits, and exciting missions were on the horizon. Consider the case of Erwin Rommel, who was not, like many others, a fanatical supporter of Nazism. In 1933, when he was forty-two years old, he was only a battalion commander, before being promoted to the rank of field marshal in 1942, thanks to Hitler's wars. To be sure, he owed this promotion to his work and talent as a leader of the armored forces but also to the growth of the army by a factor of more than fifty within a few years. An army of that size had a great need for managers. The Nazi song "Tomorrow Belongs to Me" (*Denn heute gehört uns Deutschland / und morgen die ganze Welt*) was their ideological foundation, and it held true above all for these well-trained, eager managers, both military and civilian.

In 1943, the lawyer Waldemar Ernst joked about this in an otherwise serious journal devoted to geopolitics and administrative science, comparing the English civil servant with his German counterpart. While the former traveled around the world thanks to the numerous postings offered by the British Empire, the latter thought he was embarking upon an extraordinary adventure when he moved from the Upper Rhine to the Black Forest. Now, the German could hold office from Kirkenes in Norway to Bordeaux, from Riga to Crete:[13] it was "almost unbelievable!"[14] What luck to live in such exhilarating times!

The civilian elite had been well trained: the Weimar Republic had been generous with universities and students. It helped more than any earlier German government to open up higher education, whose graduates and holders of doctorates were confronted, from 1929 on, by the prospect of unemployment caused by the economic and social crisis. The only party promising them a way out was the NSDAP (Nationalsozialistiche Deutsche Arbeiterpartei, the German National Socialist Workers' Party), which courted and recruited them, particularly in the ranks of the SS. Young people were, in fact, appointed to the highest offices in the party, though not without a struggle, first against the SA (Sturmabteilung, a paramilitary wing of the NSDAP) and its "plebeian" activists, and then within the German state in 1933, before dreaming of taking control of Europe, as early as the assault on Poland in 1939.

Among these managers, a group of academics and particularly brilliant high officials distinguished themselves by their ambitious theoretical work, notably in the pages of the journal *Reich, Volksordnung, Lebensraum* "Empire, Racial Order, Lebensraum," which they published from 1941 to 1943 under the auspices of the Institute for State Research (Institut für Staatsforschung). The publication was associated with the University of Berlin but guided by the SS and directed by the young professor Reinhard Höhn, who was also a department head in the very selective SD (Sicherheitsdienst, the SS's security service). The journal, which was thus born with the Great Empire and disappeared at the moment when the latter seemed seriously compromised, if not doomed to failure, published many contributions on the future of the civil service. The administration desirable for the Greater German Empire (*Großdeutsches Reich*) was sketched out in articles that ranged from the most general to the most specific, indeed to the most technical, as in a bracing but not exactly exhilarating piece on "file processing for planned administrative management."[15]

The eldest of the managers and editors of the journal we have been discussing was very young. Born in 1902, Wilhelm Stuckart had just celebrated his thirty-first birthday in 1933, when his party took power. A jurist who had written his doctoral dissertation on trade registers, Stuckart had been a legal consultant to the NSDAP, which he had joined in 1922, and an attorney for the SA. Along with others, such as Hans Frank, Walter Luetgebrune, and Roland Freisler, he was part of an advisory team that defended Nazi activists who had been indicted for political acts of violence. Hitler's arrival in the chancellery propelled Stuckart into the highest level of the civil service. In 1933, he was appointed director of the central headquarters and then state secretary at the Ministry of Education; in 1935, he was transferred, with the same title, to the Reich Ministry of the Interior. This outstanding technician and devoted activist appears to have been in charge of preparing two major laws: one passed in April of 1933 concerning the "restoration of the German civil service," which excluded from the latter both political enemies and Jews, and then the laws passed in September 1935, known as the "Nuremberg Laws," which redefined German nationality, depriving Jews of their citizenship and forbidding them from having sexual relations with non-Jews. A specialist of Aryanness and Aryanization, Stuckart commented on these laws in an article written with his colleague Hans Globke (who was later a close advisor to Chancellor Adenauer) to promote the strictest possible interpretation of them. He was also interested in the Reich's expansion, and, in 1938, he wrote the articles that incorporated Austria into Germany, and then, in the spring and the fall of 1939, the articles that settled the status of Bohemia and Moravia and Poland. A paragon of Nazism and anti-Semitism, he was thus also a dedicated annexationist, the archetype of the high official and intellectual of Nazi action.

It was in his capacity as a specialist in administrative organization and as a theorist of the Greater Germany conquered by German armies that Stuckart multiplied and encouraged reflections on the administration of the evolving Reich. To be sure, the time was historic and the prospects were exciting, but so many problems loomed on the horizon!

The most pressing of these problems involved human resources (*Menschenmaterial*). The increasing number of territories under German sovereignty led to a "gigantic Empire" (*Riesenreich*) that had to be administered with personnel that was not growing but rather decreasing in number, because more and more officials were in the armed forces. Stuckart made this alarming observation in his contribution to a Festschrift in honor of Heinrich Himmler on the occasion of his fortieth birthday, in 1941, at a time of great euphoria in the East.[16] It was urgent therefore, he argued, to transform the German civil service, not only for wartime, but also for the centuries of peace to come[17] in the German colonial empire founded on the ruins of a USSR whose defeat and dismemberment had been taken for granted. How could they do *more* with *fewer people*? They simply had to do *better*—and that improvement was not a question of central government, nor was it a matter of resources. Doing better with less was incumbent on the agents of the German administration, which had to reform—indeed, transform—its practices in order to confront the challenges of the present and the future. Stuckart's long article, though dense, nonetheless remained vague. Without footnotes, it was neither scientific nor demonstrative; it was purely prescriptive. It was an accumulation of assertions and injunctions to be this way, or to act that way. In this case, Stuckart vigorously advocated "elasticity, pleasure in working, proximity to life and to vitality"[18] and appealed to the "creative initiative"[19] of civil servants devoted to their task and to their mission. Every one of them had to enjoy "a vast sphere of personal responsibility, of duties of his own, of individual initiative," and had to be able to "develop himself" in the new German space, and through the work conceived therein. For that to happen (and on the condition that the central government remain strong,[20] which was indispensable in a *Führerstaat* where the driving force was vertical and everything was subordinated to the will of the *Führer*), the general organization had to be as decentralized as possible: "It corresponds to the German essence and identity" that "everything that does not absolutely have to be dealt with by the central government [. . .] must be managed in a decentralized way."[21] References to the German essence and to the decentralized nature of the Holy Roman Empire were very well-suited to promote a principle of subsidiarity that unburdened the central government and delegated a large measure of assessment and action to local administrators. According to Stuckart—who was recycling a commonplace here—the German tradition was diametrically opposed to that of France, in which civil servants, strangled by a punctilious and imperious central government, were so unhappy. A stereotype commonly found in Nazi literature suggests that France was suffering the "death of the spirit of initiative and joy in work"[22] because of an "unhealthy, pointless schematization"[23] that was "foreign to life and bureaucratic."[24]

The attorney Walter Labs, born in 1910, held a doctorate in law and was a young high-ranking official in the "Ministry of Occupied Territories in the East," where he followed the SS's genocidal policy with interest. He fervently approved of Stuckart in a 1943 article about the latter's administration. The French were not the only ones who were rigid, he wrote: the Soviets were too or at least would be until their state disappeared. The case was entirely different in Germany:

The principle of Germany's administration, on the contrary, provides for strong direction by the central government as the highest authority, but the administration's center of gravity is located at the lower levels, which are granted the greatest freedom of decision-making and individual initiative.[25]

German freedom, an ancient ethno-nationalist *topos*, is thus also developed in and through the freedom of officials and administrators in general—the freedom to obey orders and to carry out the assigned mission by any means necessary.

Stuckart, Labs, and others were repeating, albeit in more refined and carefully selected terms, what was heard everywhere, and what we have read in Backe's handbook ("Don't complain to your supervisors, don't ask them to help"): there was in fact a transfer of competencies, but not of resources, and everyone had to make do with what was available, resorting to inventiveness, "initiative," but also making use of local resources and people. What mattered was carrying out the mission, accomplishing the task.

To facilitate the administrators' work, a normative "simplification" (*Vereinfachung*) was needed, in order to clear blockages, free up energies, and prevent action from being hindered. In his great wisdom, the Führer had issued, as Walter Labs reminds us, a "decree of administrative simplification" on August 28, 1939. The title of this decree, along with its first article, tells us all we need to know: "I expect from all administrations relentless activity and rapid decisions, freed from all bureaucratic inhibitions."[26] A simplifying blow delivered in two pages, and a few explicit words: shortened deadlines, tacit agreements, freedom from supervision, personal and local initiative, a reduction in the beneficiary's rights and avenues of appeal . . . In the first issue of his own periodical, Wilhelm Stuckart already insisted on the "necessity of an elastic exercise of administration, which must not feel bound to rigid forms,"[27] and healthy decisions to allow "freer, more flexible" action[28] emancipated from any "calcified schema."[29]

The obsession with "life" and "proximity to life," "vitality" and the rejection of any procedure or system "foreign to life" may surprise us. The organic metaphor and the biological register are omnipresent. However, there is nothing astonishing in the discourse of a fervent Nazi who was certain that the time of "law" (abstract, intellectual, and dead) was over, and that that of "right" (concrete, instinctual, and living) had begun (again) in 1933. Life is flux, and any obstacle to the circulation of forces and fluids gives rise to a thrombosis that is dangerous, or even fatal, for the "race." A natural necessity governs the whole—the laws of nature that must be respected. Now, we prefer to speak of "vital forces" and the "liberation of energies" from the "norms" and "burdens" that hinder them.

Stuckart's view was endorsed by another contributor to the Himmler Festschrift: his friend and colleague Werner Best. Born in Darmstadt in 1903, the son of a postal official, he held a doctorate in law and was active in nationalist-conservative organizations that were very critical of the Nazis, though he joined the NSDAP in 1929. A member of the SD, he became one of the architects of the Gestapo, even as he continued to write legal works on the community, the police, the state, and Lebensraum.[30]

Best's observation in the article, which he entitled "Fundamental Questions for a German Administration of Greater Germany," is identical to Stuckart's: "The rapid and powerful extension of the territory on which the German people exercises its sovereignty, directly or indirectly, obliges us to rethink all the conceptions, principles, and forms in which this exercise has been conceived and constructed,"[31] to undertake "a total and profound reflection" in response to immediate challenges, but also to build the structures of the future.

Although the territory under German control was growing, "the German population was not going to be able to double the number of its public officials."[32] There too, it was a question of doing more with less, by doing better. Significantly, Werner Best appealed to prestigious predecessors by invoking the spirits of the Prussian reformers of the period between 1807 and 1813—military men and senior officials who had reacted to France's victory in 1806 by transforming, in a deep and lasting fashion, both the state and the army of the Kingdom of Prussia. The prestige of these men (Hardenberg, Stein, Humboldt, and, in military matters, Scharnhorst, Gneisenau, and Clausewitz) was due to the fact that, in the wake of these reforms, Prussia had, along with Austria and Russia, defeated the French armies at Leipzig (October 1813), as a prologue to a victorious war that culminated in the Battle of Waterloo on June 18, 1815.

A master of the art of administrative reform, Baron Karl vom und zum Stein had provided the key to optimizing public action with a maxim endorsed by Werner Best: "Government must be small, thrifty, and in the people's interest."[33] The author explains: "Thrifty government means managing everything while spending as little as possible."[34] The historical exaltation connected with the construction of the Greater German Empire thus did not exclude less noble economic and budgetary considerations: the intellectuals, administrators, and high officials who conceived Greater Germany, the expansion of the Reich and the adaptation of the state structures it required, were concerned with economizing by urging that more, much more, be done with the same, or even decreasing, resources. It was necessary to be as efficacious as ever and, confronted by the gigantic challenges of the time—which demanded an openness of mind, a rapidity of execution, and a practical flexibility at least comparable to that of the Prussian reformers of 1807—the question arose: was the state the best tool for this purpose?

CHAPTER 2
MUST THE STATE BE ABOLISHED?

The state's civil service, and the state itself, seem singularly ill-treated in the reflections that we have just reviewed, especially given that the reforming technocrats we are discussing were sometimes linked to or employed by institutions or para-state agencies such as the administration of the Four Year Plan run by Hermann Goering or the SD, the SS Reichsführer's intelligence service.

Members of the SS were particularly aware of the complexity of the situation, starting with their own position: they were senior police officials, and as members of the SD, they were funded primarily by the NSDAP's budget.

In practice, the state, threatened by a profusion of institutions and *ad hoc* organs, and above all by the party itself, seemed to be declining. Moreover, Nazi language preferred the term "movement" (*Bewegung*) to "party" (*Partei*). The "movement" embraced the dynamics of life and of history, whereas the state (*der Staat*), too loyal to its etymology, is a *status*, a stable and static institution that cannot keep up with the flow of initiatives and decisions to be made and, in the worst case, hinders them. The Third Reich's ideologues and jurists are in complete agreement: the state did not exist among the original Germans, who were organized in tribes, in families that respected the laws of nature and of life. The state is a creation of late Roman law, contemporary with the racial degeneration of ancient Rome and with the composition of the first legal codes (including the Code of Justinian), which stabilized the law on parchment, an abstract, written law, whereas the original law was a matter of pure instinct and vital drive.[35] The original German law gave way to Jewish law (weren't the Jews the People of the Law *par excellence*?), which was guaranteed by a static state and its institutions. In a parallel development, the Church, another state, established itself as the guardian of a dogma lethal for the German race (the equality of all humans and the universality of the law), while at the same time suffocating and destroying the healthy natural cults of the Germans, who were forced to convert by (Judeo-)Christians as sly as they were violent.

The genesis of the state was thus a catastrophe for the German race. Its existence and its action were equally nefarious. The German cinema of the Third Reich took pleasure in representing heroes full of genius and will, forces that confront the absurd, morbid opposition of civil servants too respectful of rules and laws that they do not question. One of these heroes was Robert Koch, the brilliant physician who discovered the tuberculosis bacillus and who, in the biopic that Goebbels's cinema devoted to him in 1939,[36] excoriates "the blessed Bureaucratius," the patron saint of a Prussian administration too persnickety and too slow for his genius. The same holds for the German colonizer Carl Peters in the eponymous film made in 1941,[37] which represents him as the brutal hero of the conquest of East Africa, battling the chicaneries of pedantic scribblers. The character of Frederick II of Prussia, in the series of films made about him at the time, teaches the same lesson: to do something great, one has to be able to laugh at the rules, free up energy, and move fast.

The creation of a professional civil service had the disastrous effect of making the rule and the state an end in itself, whereas every institution should only function as a means to an end and allow the German race to develop and spread. Adolf Hitler said the same in a speech given at the "movement's" rally in Nuremberg in 1934: "It is not the state that gives us orders, it is we who give orders to the state. It is not the state that has created us, it is we who are creating our state." The state, he wrote in *Mein Kampf*, is a "means to an end," and that end is not administrative or abstract but concrete and biological: it is the strengthening and the perpetuation of the race.

The theory is thus clear: to our great astonishment, the Nazis turn out to be absolute opponents of the state. The practice is still more explicit. Beginning in the 1940s, political analysts like Friedrich Naumann, and then historians, were intrigued by what seemed to be a paradox. Whereas the Third Reich took care to appear to be the strictest order ever, the way it functioned resembled an unstable and chaotic system more than it did the impeccable choreography of its processions. The image that the new regime projected was architectonic: the hieratic rigor of its neo-classical architecture was duplicated by the disciplined movements of human "columns," the carnal architecture reproducing the geometrical regularity of the stone. The cinematic news reports, like Leni Riefenstahl's films, hammered home this image of an implacable order: the disorder of the Weimar Republic, the chaos of democracy, was being replaced by the ordered geometry of a new Germany, unified and brought together by the will of the Führer, the interpreter of natural laws and of the deep will of the German people. The German essence, in contrast to Latin dissipation, to dark trances or Jewish anarchy, is all order and unity: *Ein Volk, ein Reich, ein Führer* (we note in passing that there is no mention of *ein Staat*).

This self-representation had the immense merit of reassuring contemporaries: a modern-day Augustus, Hitler was putting an end to the chaos of civil wars by abolishing the Republic and (re)creating the Empire, bringing to heel the "powerful columns of our movement." The Nazis' coming to power was in fact followed by what they themselves called *Gleichschaltung*, the "taming," or more precisely, the perfect synchronization of the German machine—not only society (with the elimination of any opposition) and the state (purged of its undesirable officials), but also the party (with the elimination of the SA hierarchy in particular).

Nonetheless, the functioning of the new regime was directly dependent more on chaotic improvisation and disorder than on Leni Riefenstahl's impeccably geometrical images. In addition to the coexistence of the state (whose structures, tested and damaged by purges and repression, continued to exist), and of the party, the twelve years of Nazi domination saw the multiplication of *ad hoc* organs, institutions, and agencies, to the point of rendering decision-making processes and administrative actions almost indecipherable. The preparation for war, and then the beginning of the fighting, aggravated this tendency. Who was in control of economic planning in Germany? The Reich chancellery, which had been endowed with unprecedented power since the Enabling Act of March 23, 1933? The Ministry of the Economy? The Reichsbank? The party? Or perhaps it was the administration of the Four Year Plan, created in 1936 and directed by Hermann Goering, who was also president of the Reichstag, Minister of the Air Force, Grand Jägermeister of the Reich, Prussian Minister of the Interior, head of the Luftwaffe, and no doubt that's not the full list.

Once war was declared, who was in charge of the territories conquered in Poland and then in the great expanse of the East? The Wehrmacht? The leaders of the police and the SS? The Ministry of the East, headed by Rosenberg? The Ministry of Agriculture, which was entrusted with ensuring the Reich's food supply? Goering, again, and his Four Year Plan? The Party's Gauleiters? Speer's Ministry of Armament, which was always looking for more workers? Goebbels, the plenipotentiary official responsible for the Total War Effort, starting in 1943?

Quarrels over jurisdiction were constant, as were conflicts over precedence and squabbles among party bosses. Personalities clashed, and logical frameworks collided violently, irreconcilably. To return to our example of the new territories in the East, while Himmler, the SS, and its multiple organs pursued a policy of uncompromising race war, Alfred Rosenberg and his departments at the Ministry of the East were advocating political discernment: it was necessary to remain on good terms with the racially inferior populations who were welcoming the Germans because they were opposed to Stalinism. This request for common sense—not alienating a local population that was well-disposed toward the invaders—had almost no effect on Himmler and his men, who were not inclined to see Slavs or "Asiatics" as potential political partners or, worse, as allies. A third actor, the Wehrmacht, was to react differently, recruiting numerous Soviet volunteers as combat auxiliaries without excessive respect for racial orthodoxy.

This constant conflict between minor potentates and great principles resulted in a loss of time, energy, and considerable resources. The Reich's territory suffered directly when it was invaded, and when no one knew clearly who was in charge of defending the civilian populations. What was true on the ground was also true at the highest level: Goebbels's diary, Himmler's appointment book, and Goering's and Ribbentrop's confessions all testify to the level of mutual detestation and bitter competition the regime's hierarchs very rapidly reached owing to lack of clarity. The only way of settling a question was to obtain the Führer's arbitration, and this led to a frantic struggle to gain access to his person and his favor, thus his personal secretariat, directed by Martin Bormann, acquired excessive power.

Historians and political analysts have given this improbable organization the name of "polycracy": what characterizes the Third Reich is in fact the multiplicity of instances of power and decision-making, along with incessant rivalry. At first, the observation is surprising: "German rigor" and "taste for order" are not present, and still less the "totalitarian" logic of unity and verticality.

Interpreting the phenomenon is all the more delicate. This institutional disorder has been seen as the result of feverish haste: indeed the Nazis never ceased to say that Germany and the German people had lost too much time, that a race against history, decadence, and degeneration had begun and it was necessary to act quickly and achieve a great deal. Spontaneous initiatives were multiplied without taking the time to coordinate and supervise them. The other plausible reason is the tendency toward the development of personal fiefs, carved out by each party official, at every level, under the indolent, wily oversight of a "weak dictator" who often acted like a feudal lord and let develop individual initiatives of which he would occasionally approve. This interpretation in terms of feudal administration is interesting: from the Gauleiters to the ministers of the Reich, each defended his territory and his jurisdiction—the most powerful succeeding in creating institutions they controlled, like Goering or Rosenberg, who had a personal administration that bore his name: the Einsatzstab Reichsleiter Rosenberg. It kept an eye on, among other things, the organized pillaging of the European continent's artistic and cultural resources, an enterprise that conflicted with the activities of the chancellery (for the "Führer's" Museum in Linz), of Goering (for his personal collection), and of Himmler's chancellery (for the Ahnenerbe, the SS's think tank). Even as they engaged in pillaging, predation, and theft, the Nazis practiced constant disorganization and the battle of each against all.

In this competition between parallel organs assigned to the same mission and the same territories, we can also see a form of spontaneous, unconscious administrative Darwinism. If the state, with its geometrical organization, its inertia, and its immutable rules, is incapable of coping with the biological and historical emergencies of the time, the metastatic proliferation of individual initiatives and the development of institutional rivalry can result in the quickest and most radical solutions. Starting in 1933, the slow evolution and the regulated organization of the state were in fact replaced by confrontation between ambitions and a frantic attempt to win the Führer's favor, which everyone thought could be obtained by interpreting his words and his ideas as radically as possible. The history of the Third Reich's anti-Jewish policy can certainly be understood in light of this fact. The principles are as firm as they are vague, as shown by famous slogans such as *Juden raus!* ("out with the Jews!"), which were local initiatives on the part of zealous local Gauleiters, and by the hasty activities of agencies and committees that led to the harshest decisions, to the great satisfaction of the chancellery. Kristallnacht provides a good example: on the evening of November 9, 1938, Goebbels caught everyone off guard by ordering reprisals against German Jews following the assassination of a German diplomat in Paris. In doing so, he pleased the SA's local units, which were glad to see a little action, thoroughly satisfied Hitler, and forced Himmler and Heydrich to support his decision. From 1941 on, the Shoah can also be seen through the prism of administrative Darwinism: local initiatives, competing among themselves, won the central government's approval in the framework of a cumulative radicalization which, from the point of view of Hitler, Himmler, Goebbels, and others such as Robert Ley, the head of the German Labor Front and a rabid anti-Semite, was in principle virtuous.

Using the phrase of a German senior official of the time, Ian Kershaw has clearly stressed the will of the Reich's organs to "work towards the Führer" (*dem Führer entgegenarbeiten*), to fulfill his alleged desires. Polycracy, through its administrative Darwinism, constituted a system and took on a particular meaning, a place in the Nazi "worldview" that was ultimately logical: life is a battle, the world is the battlefield, and the war is between races, between agencies, and between the central government and the agencies.

Polycracy was conceived, in real time, by certain jurists and senior officials who were passionately interested in questions of organization. Its functioning was thoroughly theorized, or supported by theory, through a juridical and administrative line of thought that advocated a different conception of the state—depreciating and reducing it to a simple agency like any other, or even doing away with it entirely.

The Nazis' depreciation of the state is explicit, as we have seen above. The state ceases to be the supreme authority, the organ of sovereignty, and becomes a means to an end, a biological end in this case: it is subordinated to race, of which it is only the servant and the instrument. The only truly perennial entity that is stable in the sense of the Latin *stare*, the only existence destined to be perpetuated and projected into eternity, is not the state, which is an artifact created by Jews, but race, an indestructible biological reality. This depreciation of the state was accompanied by nullifying reflections on its origin and functions. It was also accompanied by commentaries and practices hostile to the ethos of civil servants, who were bogged down in rules, incapable of undertaking "initiatives," and deaf to the emergencies of the moment. In judicial matters, the question is particularly clear: to avoid being dependent on judges and their alleged laxity, the Nazi "movement" instituted a permanent, exceptional state of emergency, endowing the police, in orders issued in February 1933, with exorbitant powers in the area of political repression. An individual who was discharged and avoided prison could be confined in a concentration camp by police orders without the judge's supervision. On April 26, 1942, the Reichstag gave the "Führer and chancellor of the Reich" the power to terminate and fire any official, including magistrates, whose acts and decisions were not in conformity with historical and biological necessities. An excessively scrupulous official who wanted to respect the rules of legal procedure, or a magistrate who didn't decapitate enough, might be dismissed without possibility of appeal.

Under the Third Reich, the state, like its servants, no longer had inalienable dignity. A means of political decision-making like any other, it was in competition—and this must be emphasized—with a myriad of *ad hoc* administrations that had the status of what has, since the nineteenth century, been called "agencies," that is, organs endowed with a mission, a project, and a budget to carry out that mission, and whose existence is limited to the duration of the task at hand. These agencies increased in number after 1933, especially to accomplish missions connected with war: that was the case for the Four Year Plan created in 1936, though its existence was prolonged beyond 1940 as the Todt Organization, which was created in 1938 by the engineer Fritz Todt, to carry out many small and large projects for the Reich, ranging from building barracks in *Stalags* to building the Atlantic Wall. We could also mention the Reich Commissariat for the Strengthening of the German Race *(Reichskommissariat für die Festigung deutschen Volkstums*, RKF), which was created in 1939 and assigned to Himmler. The RKF's mission, under the direction of a professor of agricultural geography at the University of Berlin, Konrad Meyer, was to draw up a plan for the general colonization of the territories of the East, a mission that ended up developing several successive versions of the General Plan for the East from 1940 to 1943. The proliferation of these organs, of which there were dozens, raises questions. To be sure, jurists specializing in public law had been reflecting on agencies since the nineteenth century, in both Germany and in France, where the question was how institutions that were not *stricto sensu* state organs could respond to the specific technical needs of the nascent industrial age. In the nineteenth century, the creation of such agencies did not call into question the very principle of the existence of the state, whereas it was undoubtedly undermined by their multiplication under the Third Reich.

One of the jurists most involved in this reflection was Reinhard Höhn, a specialist in public law who, in the grand tradition of that area, was especially excited about history and sociology. He was initially close to Carl Schmitt, whom he assiduously courted without receiving the intellectual recognition that he expected from the master of studies in constitutional law and public law in Germany. Then he radically distinguished himself from Schmitt by his historical deconstruction and legal depreciation of the notion of the state—which was particularly visible in a work published in 1934 entitled *Die Wandlung im staatsrechtlichen Denken* (*The Change in Thinking about Constitutional Law*).[38]

In this book, Höhn carries out a historical reinterpretation of the concept of the state to show that it is obsolete. According to him, the notion of the state is inseparable from the domination of the sovereign princes of the modern era, which appeared in Italy during the Renaissance and achieved a brilliant maturity in the France of Richelieu and Louis XIV. Consubstantial with an age of the individual (a prince or political figure) that was now over, the state was no longer relevant in the time and in the era of the "community."

Obsessed with power and domination, the Italian *podestà* and then the French absolute monarchs created, with the state, an instrument that served them. Legal theory created an illusion and made people believe the state was something other than an instrument of domination: it was hypostatized as an "invisible person" and transformed into a perennial instance of sovereignty, whereas, according to Höhn, it was really nothing more than an "apparatus" (*Apparat*) in the service of the established power. In the context of the "national revolution" that had just been carried out, it was appropriate to make use of this state, of this "apparatus of agencies and officials,"[39] while remaining very aware of what it was and what it was not, or what it was no longer: "it is no longer in the service of the sovereign prince or some undefined general interest, but serves the people in the form of the community of the people."[40] That is precisely how the Nazis seized control of it: "The movement took possession of the state and assigned new tasks to it."[41]

In a chapter of the anthology entitled *Fundamental Questions Regarding the Concept of Law*[42] which he co-edited in 1938, Höhn completed his redefinition of the state:

> The state is no longer the supreme political entity [. . .]. Rather, it is limited to the performance of missions that are assigned to it by the leadership (*Führung*) in the service of the community of the people. In this sense, it is now no more than a simple means that can be used and whose objectives and action are assigned to it.[43]

The decline of the state is stunning: formerly a majestic and revered authority, especially in Prussia and in Germany, where before 1933 the cult of public service and officialdom, and of the army, was not an empty phrase, it is reduced to the status of one tool among others. Significantly, "leadership" is distinct and distant from the state; it refers less to the political leadership of the state than to the authority of command, of direction or management, of the community of the people that assigns this or that mission to the state, among other authorities, organs, or agencies.

A late institution imported by the evangelization of the Germanic tribes, the state is antithetical to German liberty and to its free development, and still more since the princes' absolutist project appropriated it as an instrument in the service of royal sovereignty. Höhn did not change his view or his doctrine after 1945: he had been an enemy of the state, and he remained one. In a work published in 1970, he lamented the fact that the "bond of mutual fidelity" characteristic of the medieval period had become a "bond of uniliteral obedience": the "feudal lords" of the Middle Ages and the "members of guilds" had become "subjects of the absolute state."[44] They were forbidden to "argue" in front of the prince, the incarnation of sovereignty—Louis XIV's famous apocryphal remark (*"L'État, c'est moi,"* "I am the state") never fails to be cited in the argumentation.[45] For Höhn, everything "that is done" in the army, the administration, and society, "must have been ordered" beforehand. As a good lawyer, Höhn is a nominalist, and confounds the word ("absolutism") with the thing, the discourse and the practice. What makes the "machine" work is not consent, support, or enthusiasm, but "the fear of punishment." The long history of authority and subjection is conflated with the history of the state.

In the Third Reich, these days were over. They were also over after 1945. A mode of *Menschenführung* adapted to the spirit of the twentieth century and to the German essence—which was free by nature—had to be theorized and implemented.

Chapter 3
"German Liberty"

The Nazis' rejection of the state and their repudiation of its very existence may be surprising, so much do we take it for granted that "totalitarianism" presupposes a "totalitarian state." However, in the eyes of all the thinkers, ideologues, theorists, and "combat intellectuals" in the Nazi movement, the state, far from being merely useless, was also harmful and even disastrous.

Once again, as almost always, the Nazis drew on a tradition and a heritage: on Social Darwinism, on racism, and on the eugenics of the second half of the nineteenth century, three cultural and ideological movements that prospered in a synergy that proved devastating for a portion of humanity—those that were considered failed, corrupt, and "unworthy of living."

From the Social Darwinism arising from Herbert Spencer's ultra-liberal reflections, the Nazis inherited the idea that the state hinders, or even wholly blocks, the logic and the dynamics of nature. The latter, as is well known, allows individuals that are not viable to perish. But because of its activity of redistributing wealth, and because of the early system of public health insurance established in Germany, the state ensures the survival of those who are not viable. Contrary to the implacable—and healthy—logic of "natural selection," which, in the human milieu, takes the form of social selection, the state takes on a counter-selective or anti-selective role that causes the sick and the incapable, that is, the unhealthy, to prosper at the expense of the healthy. As early as the 1880s, Chancellor Bismarck, inspired by the Protestant pietists' doctrines of justice, but also by the socialists, whom he was eager to wipe out by drying up their electoral base, had established in Germany what the Nazis and Social Darwinists considered a highly problematic system of public health insurance: the unemployed, those professional loafers, were encouraged in their vice instead of being abandoned to their fate—that is to a reinvigorating famine that would finally teach them to live and to work. As for "hereditary invalids," they were protected by legislation that, contrary to established scientific opinion, allowed, indeed demanded, their survival, growth, and multiplication. Whereas healthy, hard-working German families lived in their poverty-stricken slums, individuals with Down's syndrome and hydrocephalus, as well as paraplegics, were prospering in luxurious hospices that were, of course, usually financed by private charities, but encouraged by the state through legislation that was anti-natural because it was counter-selective. On this subject, Nazi propaganda was inexhaustible.

Let what must die, die, said the Social Darwinists and their Nazi disciples: that holds for unprofitable activity as well as for minds and bodies that are "unproductive."

Unfortunately, the state is the artificial institution that causes the ink of the law to triumph over the blood of the race, and artifice over nature: by insisting on the survival and the multiplication of the weak, the useless, and the losers, the state promotes a gangrene that will prove fatal, in the end, for "the body of the people" (*Volkskörper*). This organicist metaphor designating the "community of the people" is in reality so literal that it is no longer a metaphor.

The state is all the more harmful and disastrous because it seems to take a malicious pleasure in hindering and suffocating "living forces" by means of persnickety regulations implemented by all the unimaginative pen-pushers and the servile eunuchs that populate the civil service: this reglementary clot, and this administrative infection, coagulate the blood, the flows and dynamics of the Germanic race, instead of fluidifying them and encouraging their circulation. Under such conditions, thrombosis is inevitable, and death is certain if a salutary change in direction is not made. The multiple calls to "simplify" rules and norms, the incessant condemnations of any "bureaucratic spirit," the violent stigmatization of civil servants and judges who still insist on applying the law—all that proceeds from the Social Darwinist heritage and is part of an ideal liberation of Germanness, which is still too hindered by laws written and promulgated by Jews.

In its domestic affairs, the state is thus what hobbles and enslaves the German race: static, it denies the dynamics of life; general, indeed universal, it is not in the service of the particular (racial identity); artificial, it denies nature. It is the dead seizing control of the living.

If it did not have all these flaws, the state would still remain useless: the Germanic race, which knows by instinct how to govern itself by respecting the law of nature (procreate, fight, rule), that is, the only *law* that matters, has no need to be subordinated to a transcendent institution that ensures civil peace and sees to it that rules are respected. Since every member of the good race has a healthy mind and respects the natural norm, peace reigns, children are born, and bodies are nourished. "Codes" (civil and criminal) are superfluous because public order proceeds from a pre-established harmony among Germanic bodies, hearts, and minds. Every racially healthy person can only be a Nazi and adhere to the Führer's orders, which are, ultimately, the commands of life itself. The community of race is necessarily a community of body and soul: in this healthy universe, the state, as an institution guaranteeing the common good, is completely useless. Individuals behave naturally as genuine *members* of the "*body* of the people," because they all share the same blood and common sense. The Leviathan state, that clumsy mammoth, can and must be replaced by agencies that will evolve—just as much as individuals will—in a harmony pre-established by nature, from which they will draw the ability to make speedy decisions and execute them flexibly.

In foreign affairs, the state is revealed to be just as superfluous. Conceived since the seventeenth century not only as the guarantor of civil peace but also as the site of sovereignty with regard to other states—a view established by the international order following the Peace of Westphalia in 1648—the state, in the Nazis' conception of space and species, of biotopes and races, is no longer necessary; quite the contrary. The international order is doomed to disappear, because there are no nations, only races. In this zoological universe, an essentially superior race is destined to dominate by destruction, enslavement, or at least the exploitation of other races: "international law," "international order," "nations," and "states" are all obsolete concepts and realities that will soon be dead. The days of the League of Nations, of interstate diplomacy and nation-states, are numbered, because the advent of the Greater Germany that Stuckart, Best, Höhn, and their friends dreamed about is near.

The state, in the Nazis' strictest conception of it, had only a few decades to live, over the course of a transitional phase marked by war and the gradual advent of the only valid order, the natural, biological-racial order, and of *Lebensraum*, the nourishing biotope of the Germanic race. In the foreign order—which was destined, sooner or later, to merge with the domestic order because the *Lebensraum* of the Germanic race had to be expanded to the whole of the continent—the subsistence of a German state still served to regulate exchanges with other European nation-states until they were absorbed into the Reich's *Lebensraum*, that is, until the advent of Nazi rule. The term *Reich*, we must remember, does not mean "state" and does not even imply a state's existence: as the Nazis used it, *Reich* returns to the medieval, religious meaning of *regnum*—rule, era, and area—to the detriment of its juridical-institutional meaning which, in the modern period, referred to the state's institutions.

Doomed to a gradual disappearance in the international order, the state, in domestic matters, had to be hollowed out little by little to the benefit of agencies destined to multiply in order to assume, in a "dynamic" and not "bureaucratic" manner, its sovereign missions. Pending this necessary disintegration, the state could still be tolerated on the condition that it take on a pro-selective role. The state, during the decades that remained to it, had the right to live only insofar as it no longer hobbled nature but rather encouraged it. Counter-selective up to that point, because it protected the weak and the ill, it had to become the rigorous and exclusive auxiliary of nature through eugenicist prophylactic legislation (sterilization of "hereditary invalids," "asocial individuals," "the indolent," and other "deviants"), and even through lethal practices (gassing, then euthanasia by injection, of the "unsuccessful," "unproductive" and "unprofitable"). As the auxiliary of nature, the state had to *let people die*, or rather, *cause them to die* by guaranteeing, or even hastening, necessary processes—for there was no alternative to the apodictic law of nature. The welfare state was thus to succumb—as soon as possible—to biological necessity. What about the police state? Nineteenth-century liberals tolerated it without difficulty, since the public use of force, a sovereign prerogative like coining money and the monopoly on waging war, ensured an order and stability that were indispensable for the exercise of individual liberties and the proper functioning of business. But the police state also had no future in the Nazi universe: sooner or later, the spontaneous harmony of a pure, homogeneous racial community would make any delinquency *naturally* impossible. What healthy member of the "community of the people" would think of stealing an old lady's purse or robbing a bank? The role to be assigned to the SS, after the "final victory," was thus more military than police-oriented: veterans and units on active duty would guard the "borderlands" of the Empire, at the foot of the Urals, in order to keep at bay "Asiatic" and "Mongoloid" hordes that might be tempted to make raids on Germanic territory. Within the *Volksgemeinschaft*, order would be immanent and spontaneous, and the rare, good-natured excesses of festive parties would be looked upon with paternal benevolence by the NSDAP's local authorities or, at worst, set right by a salutary beating administered by members of the Hitler Youth or the SA. In the meantime, fifteen or twenty years of eugenics, prophylactic police work, and war would have eliminated criminal germs, under the guidance of the party, its organizations, and agencies—the SA, the SS, Hitler Youth, the BDM (Bund deutscher Mädel, League of German Girls), the NSV (Nationalsozialistische Volkswohlfahrt, National Socialist Mutual Aid Society), the NSKK (Nationalsozialistiches Kraftfahrkorps, the NSDAP's fleet of motorized vehicles), T4, etc.—and not the incurable police state, ethically incapable of coping with its public function and deaf to the pressing imperatives of biology.

Loosening the state's straitjacket, ensuring the reign of nature and respect for the law of blood, and liberating the good initiatives with necessarily lively force would bring about a full and complete "Germanic liberty."

This theme of "German liberty" is an old ethno-nationalist *topos* that was adopted by both foreigners and Germans. The Germanness of the forests never witnessed despotism or dictatorship, according to the Roman historian Tacitus in his *Germania*. Acquainted with the terrifying Germania only by hearsay, Tacitus reported that the tribes there governed themselves by discussion and common decision in assemblies called *Things*—an archaic word resuscitated by the Third Reich's *Thingstätten*, Greek-style amphitheaters designed for choral theatrical shows, dozens of which were built from 1933 on.

This "freedom of the forests" was celebrated by all those

who, in the modern era, were opposed to the absolute power of the princes, like Boulainvilliers in the seventeenth century, or Montesquieu in the eighteenth. Johann Gottlieb Fichte, in his *Discourses to the German Nation*, published during the French occupation of Prussia after the defeat of 1806, also attached great importance to this liberty that was both original and essential. The French, he wrote, were a mixture of Germanic, Latin, and Gallic; only the Germans had remained self-identical over the centuries, spoke an authentic language, and were free by essence—the French being only the subjects of a tyrant, Napoleon, who was a worthy successor of the Roman Caesars, the popes, and the absolute monarchs.

Was the Germanic man truly free? History seems to suggest something entirely different: from the all-important drills of the Prussian army to the militarism of Wilhelmine society, everything beyond the Rhine appears to be nothing but constraint and punishment. All that was very normal and perfectly explainable, commented the head of the SS, Heinrich Himmler, in a collective volume on the German police published in 1936 by his faithful jurists, Werner Best and Reinhard Höhn. For the man who was now head of the "German police," recently unified at the level of the Reich, German history had been so hard and troubled, the German people so victimized by a world of enemies primed to attack it (at that point, it had been unable to defend itself because it was incurably divided), that when it emerged from the Middle Ages, Germany had not had time to develop human types other than the soldier and the civil servant, who were arrogant and brutal, and suited, by their harshness, only to discipline excessively dissolute Germans:

> We Germans must be clear on this point: we have no self-assured knights or gentlemen like other countries where Germanic peoples live [. . .]. We have not been able to develop these types. That takes centuries of peace, without

being disturbed [. . .] Therefore, we Germans threw ourselves into regulations, and it is in regulations that, through an order and discipline that we stubbornly imposed on ourselves, we have developed the two types that are the civil servant and the soldier.[46]

Everything changed in 1933. Centuries of division and weakness came to an end at the moment when, through divine Providence, Hitler came to power. In every regard, the advent of the Nazi reign provided a historic opportunity for peace and prosperity, for union and harmony, that permitted the Germanic people to live in accord with their nature—proud and free.

Reinhard Höhn says exactly that when, in one work after another, he makes himself the critical, not to say devastating, historian of the state. The state was born essentially in the modern age, at a time when the conception of dominant power opposed the prince to the subject (*Untertan*[47]—literally: someone placed below), or as summarized by Jean Bodin, whom Höhn quotes in French: "one is the lord, the other is the servant."[48] In this, Höhn sees the triumph of juridical individualism: the individual who is the prince dominates absolutely a group of subordinate individuals (the subjects), whereas the state itself is seen by juridical theory as a moral person, and hence also as an individual. Höhn argues, along with so many of his colleagues, that the individual, the new foundation of law— private as well as public—erased the "community" that was formerly the German's very reality—the family, the parish, the guild, every form of association based on natural necessity and on the whole, not on the part. The diametrical opposite of the princely state of the age of absolute monarchy, the traditional "Germanic state" was "a system of communities"[49] that had no absolute prince or despot, enlightened or not. This happy period ended forever with the advent of the modern age, at the time when the disastrous French model of a centralized, administrative, and rigid state spread to Germanic lands in the wake of the influence, prestige, and victories of Louis XIV, an absolutist monster and a tutor for despots.

In opposition to this alienation and denaturation of the German essence and German life, the jurists most fully integrated into SS groups proposed a return to the original German community, whose most authentic expression was found in the medieval period, before French political modernity, reinforced by the activity of the Church and the importation of Roman law, put an end to this original paradise. The National Socialist "community of the people" put an end to the reign of the individual—of the individual prince and the individual state, but also of the individual citizen, selfish and alone.

This return to the communitarian conception of law and the Germanic people is the proof of each person's freedom: "The principle of the community is directly opposed to the individualist principle of the sovereign princely state. We no longer govern [. . .] we lead."[50]

The person who "leads" (*führt*) is the *Führer*, and Hitler directs that mission for the simple reason that, having emerged from the ranks of the people and having understood the laws of nature and history, he is capable of deciding what the German people wants, usually through intuition: "Adolf Hitler is not a sovereign prince, he is the *Führer* and consequently cannot have subjects, but only companions who follow him."[51] The old opposition, which dated from absolutism, between prince and subject, gives way to the *Führer-Genosse* (leader-companion) pair, which is incompatible with a relationship of domination or political servitude: "It is in it that the will of the community is shaped [. . .]. In that, he is not a dictator, because what he decides emanates from the spirit of the community."[52]

What is true politically (with regard to German citizens) is also true in the administrative domain (with regard to civil servants)[53] and in the economic domain (with regard to employees).

With the revival of community spirit at the time of the "national revolution" of 1933, the Germanic man recovered his freedom on all levels of his life and activity; he is no longer subject to the abstract rigidity of the "government" inherited from the age of princes, but instead participates fully, via the *Führer*'s decision that reflects his will, in popular sovereignty: wherever "the community of the people is the point of departure, there is no longer any government, but only leadership (*es wird geführt*)."[54]

In the economic domain, that was one of the messages of the 1937 film *The Master* (*Der Herrscher*),[55] directed by Veit Harlan, in which the actor Emil Jannings plays the aging head of the Clausen Works, a large munitions firm. This exemplary boss, who has risen through the ranks to become a true *Führer*, decides at the end of the film to bequeath the Clausen Works to the "community of the people." His legacy will be handled by another worker from the workshop, not by one of the members of his family, who are self-interested parasites, indecent vultures who are all feverishly waiting for his impending death.

In Clausen's plant, workers are *led* (*geführt*), and hence free, because they serve the interest of the "productive community" which itself serves the "community of the people," as can be seen in several striking monologues delivered by Matthias Clausen and written by the politically formidable pen of Thea von Harbou, who, unlike her ex-husband Fritz Lang, had not left Germany.

The Clausen Works is presented as the archetype of what, under the Third Reich, was called a *Betriebsgemeinschaft*—the community of bosses and workers within the company. The *Betriebsgemeinschaft* is to the economic domain what the *Volksgemeinschaft* is to the political domain: a community of people without classes or class struggle. Within the company, there exist only racial brothers; there are no longer any class enemies. Everyone, both bosses and subordinates, works freely and joyfully for the common good, that of the community of the people, of the Germanic race, and of the Reich. The age of Marxism, a Jewish doctrine, is over: the innate and spontaneous unity of the German people cannot be denied or destroyed by syndicalists and left-wing ideologues, those preachers of lies and divisions.

Thus, the Reich is, in every regard and in every domain, the reign of freedom. The *Führer* is not a dictator, and still less a despot. Through his person, his career, and his actions, he is the embodiment of Germanic liberty. He commands, not by inheritance, birth, or governmental or divine decree, but because he is the person who has best understood the laws of nature and history, and is, consequently, the best qualified to protect and proliferate German blood. At all these levels, the myriad military, paramilitary, political, economic, and civilian *Führers* are also nature's chosen, designated by their gifts and their talents. Those who follow (the *Gefolgschaft*) are free, because the leaders' orders express the profound will and the necessities of the Germanic race's destiny.

In the 1980s, the historian Dieter Rebentisch clearly discerned and emphasized that the Third Reich gradually abandoned "administration" (*Verwaltung*) as too Roman and French, and resolutely entered into a managerial age characterized by fluid and proactive *Menschenführung*.[56] *Verwaltung* was part of the past age of princely states and individuals subjected to a rule they had not chosen or approved. It was the deplorable legacy of the late Roman Empire, a veritable racial sewer that was founded only on the most rigid written and general norm, of the clerical tyranny that flowed from it, and of French despotism. *Menschenführung*, on the contrary, presupposed that the community of the members of the civil service, of the company, etc. freely approved of the order and the decision-making and made them its own, adhering to principles and working of its own free will. The Third Reich was therefore not a despotic regime, but rather, as one of its jurists, Hans Frank, insisted, "a National Socialist state of law" that perfected and completed German liberty.

Before 1933, the reign of *Verwaltung* signed and sealed the servitude of the German subject, who was subjected to the mechanical, rigid structure of the state, the army, and the judicial system. The managerial age of *Menschenführung* ensured that each person could, by being *geführt* (led, guided), participate in the *Führer*'s will and freedom—that is, the will and freedom of the man who had best understood and implemented the deep will of the Germanic race and reconciled it with itself and with its nature. That held for the fundamental principles of the National Socialist community, and also, in a practical and concrete way, at the level of economic organization and everyday life.

Reinhard Höhn was proud to note that the Third Reich subverted, through the community and through freedom, the contemporary state inherited from the absolutist period. Loyal to what his colleagues were writing between 1933 and 1945 about the state, its necessary mutations and its indispensable transformation, Höhn never gave up, even after the Nazi regime ended. The problem was the state, which, since Louis XIV in France and the soldier-king in Prussia, had enslaved the beautiful German way of life instead of letting it spread and develop. After 1945, and all through his very long career as a lawyer and high SS official who had moved over to management, he never ceased, as we have seen, to repeat that since the "community of the people" was no longer on the agenda after the Reich's unconditional surrender, it was the company, with its community of colleagues, that became the sole site of freedom, of creativity, and of fulfillment.

CHAPTER 4
THE NAZI MANAGEMENT OF HUMAN RESOURCES

The Nazi jurists' theoretical work on "leading people," *Menschenführung*, a Germanized translation of the American term "management," is inextricably linked to one particular ambition and obsession: to put an end to "class war" through the unity of race and through common work in the interest of Germany and the *Volksgemeinschaft* ("the community of the people"). The idea of humans as a society composed of individuals and shot through with class conflicts is, according to the Nazis, an aberration due to French revolutionaries and those who inspired them (chiefly Rousseau), along with Karl Marx and German and Russian Judeo-Bolsheviks.

The Labor Day celebration on May 1, 1933 provided an opportunity, during a grandiose ceremony held in Berlin-Tempelhof, to proclaim the end of class warfare and the advent of a society of "race comrades" (*Volksgenossen*) united in the battle that Germany had to wage in order to survive.

The Nazi view of the world and history is dark: life is a constant battle against nature, against sickness, against other peoples and other races. This Social Darwinist *topos* was radicalized and repeated under the Third Reich in a Germany that had been severely shaken by one trauma after another: rapid and brutal modernization from 1871 to 1914, World War I (1914–18/19) and defeat, the quasi-civil war between 1918 and 1923, hyper-inflation in 1922 and 1923, and then, again, the great economic, social, and political crisis—along with a cultural and psychological crisis—that started in 1929. Thus, certain events in recent history made the siege-mentality representation of a Germany threatened on all sides more plausible, and the Nazis knew that their fear-mongering and denunciatory discourse resounded with their contemporaries' experience.

The Nazis' discourse was all the more effective because it was not limited to lamentation: it also proposed "solutions," in a Social Darwinist logic blended with racism and eugenics that the people, once again, completely accepted. For the German people to survive in this hostile world, hardness (*Härte*) and health (*Heil*) had to be combined to make the *Volksgenossen* as "efficient" as possible. The term *leistungsfähig*, omnipresent at the time, can be translated as "efficient," but also as "productive" or "profitable." The word *Leistung* refers, first of all, to an action, the act of doing something, but also to doing a lot of it (productivity) and to doing it intensely (profitability). *Leistung*, like work, is a matter of race. In his most famous book, *Race and the Soul*,[57] Professor Ludwig Ferdinand Clauß, a leading authority on psychology and racial theory, asserted that only the Germanic man was a being of action, work, and achievement (*Leistungsmensch*). Non-Germanic races expected to be saved and sustained by others, by an illusory transcendence, or by their own death, sublimated by a questionable eternal life. The German, on the contrary, came to grips with his existence and transformed nature to ensure his survival. This *topos* was hammered home by the anti-Semitic films made by the Ministry of Propaganda: Jews, those incurable Orientals, had been put to work by the German occupiers everywhere the Reich's armies had triumphed. The German, that "Prometheus of humanity" (Hitler), had forged the world, created all its culture, agriculture, and industry. Hence, all this was a matter of race, but also of the era. In *The Worker* (*Der Arbeiter*), published in 1932, Ernst Jünger noted and paid tribute to the advent of a new human type, urban, industrial, and gregarious, which, as a result of the great productive structures issuing from the industrial revolution and reinforced by World War I, planning and "total mobilization," definitively supplanted the aristocrat and the bourgeois—that is, the individual as the value, principle, and goal of social organization. Modernity was clearly a matter of fire and steel, a forge producing the new man, a warrior in the trenches, a worker in the factories, and an onlooker in the streets and the leisure industry.

Jünger, who was later to distance himself from many aspects of Nazism, agreed with it on every point it had in common with the "conservative revolution" that he himself was advocating: in a radically disillusioned world reduced to the immanence of materials, trade, and money, the individual had no value in and of himself—except in the case, which was rare, of the hero. The German man drew his meaning and his life from the group that had brought him into the world and ensured his survival: the "community of the people." Only the meaningless individual's labor in the service of the national or racial community made him worthy of living.

For the Nazis and all those who shared their way of thinking, the Germanic man was the man of the "community" (*Gemeinschaft*) and "work" (*Arbeit*). He was concerned with *producing* objects (weapons or food, for instance) and children, so as to *return* to the "community of the people" what it gave him (childcare, upbringing . . .) and to do so a hundred times over by being *efficient*. If necessary, this efficiency must be strengthened by chemical means, another remarkable achievement of the German genius: the massive consumption of methamphetamines, in the form of the Pervitin pills prescribed for workers and soldiers to increase the time they remained awake, their psychological acuity, and their physical presence, testifies to this.

This view of the individual—who does not exist in himself, since "the individual is nothing, his people is everything"—is simultaneously utilitarian and reifying. It transforms every person into a thing (*res*), into an object, that has to be useful to have the right to live and exist. The Germanic individual becomes a tool, a material (*Menschenmaterial*), and a factor—a factor in production, in growth, and in prosperity.

Nazi racism is eugenic: it is not enough to have the right blood and the right skin color; one also has to be fully employable as a productive and reproductive apparatus. Since a general pre-natal prognosis did not then exist, the Nazis relied on diagnosistics: all those considered to be hereditary invalids had to be excluded from the procreative cycle (with 400,000 forced sterilizations between 1933 and 1945), or even killed, as was the case from the beginning of the war in 1939 within the framework of the T4 operation and its successors, with 200,000 "invalids" dead by 1945. As we see, crimes against humanity and mass murder targeted biology or, literally, the "Germanic" biomass, when the latter was considered unsatisfactory or deficient. "Inefficient," "unproductive," or "unprofitable" beings (*leistungsunfähige Wesen*) are "people unworthy of living" (*lebensunwürdige Menschen*), merely "empty human shells" (*leere Menschenhülsen*) who had to be excluded from the "German genetic heritage" (*deutsche Erbmasse*). Physicians had even fewer scruples about collaborating in this bio-genetic—or, to use the terms of a Nazi jurist, "bionomic"—engineering enterprise when they saw the subject to be treated not as an individual but as the "body" of the "community of the people" as a whole, of which individuals are only parts.

The Nazi biological prism thus deforms not only aliens, those who are foreign to the race or who are seen as inferior or dangerous, but also German humanity itself, since it has to prove its excellence—in 1945, Hitler did not hesitate to say that since the Germans had lost the war, the totality of his people might well perish because of its proven inferiority.

Social, biological, and medical engineering violently attacked not only "inefficient beings" and "entities unworthy of living," but also the "asocial"—vagabonds, dreamers, unusual people in general whose existence was not yet "profitable" for the "community of the people." Starting in 1936, several operations carried out by the police and the SS rounded up thousands of people who were idle, or allegedly so, and sent them to labor camps or concentration camps.

Therefore, the German man could be neither ill, nor idle, nor involved in opposition to the new power. As a procreator, he had to have a sound constitution and maintain it by hygiene and athletic activity in order to become as hardened by work as he would be by war. We have shown elsewhere that the triptych procreate-combat-rule sums up the German's historic mission and his biological vocation. Production, through work, is one of the modalities of this combat, and all the more in a strategic context in which economic production is oriented by and toward the war to come. In 1933, and even more starting in 1936, the German economy was put in battle order for a war that was supposed to begin in 1940 at the earliest. The reorientation of production was qualitative (towards arms and their components) but also quantitative (a great deal had to be produced). What was demanded of German workers in heavy industries, in the chemical industry, and from producers of electrical components, etc., was considerable[58] in terms of the physical and temporal investment. At the highest levels of the party and the state, people were well aware that this exceptional effort to produce required counterparts. The danger of seeing a political revolution break out for social and economic reasons was one of the *Führung*'s nightmares: from the 1884 Silesian weavers' revolt, which was praised by Heinrich Heine and celebrated by the socialist poet Käthe Kollwitz, to the revolution in 1918, passing by way of the revolt of 1848, uprisings had economic causes. To avoid repeating them, any instances of famine—which were decisive in the cases just mentioned—and any exhaustion at work had to be prevented. The German people also had to be shown that they were not working in vain. Slavery happened to other peoples: the "Bolshevik paradise" was presented in countless speeches, films, images, and expositions, as an immense, open-air gulag where the Soviet "citizen," a new *mujik* crushed by production quotas and collapsing under the crack of the whip, was dying to construct canals, factories, and dams for the sole benefit of a new aristocracy, that of the "Jewish" *nomenklatura* that had dominated the country since 1917. The specter of communism, which was constantly brandished by Nazi propaganda, performed a fundamental function in Germans' psychic economy after 1933: it showed them, and proved to them, that though people worked hard in Germany, the horror was elsewhere. According to the press and political speeches, which here, as often, merely developed ancient cultural traditions and well-anchored prejudices, Soviet despotism was the contemporary avatar of "Asia's" and the "Orient's" long-standing antipathy toward freedom. Hegel already made the Orient the site of slavery (where a single person—the Persian king or the pharaoh—was free, while everyone else was enslaved), and he made Germania the site of liberty (where everyone is free thanks to the law). These commonplaces of German cultural heritage were repeated and radicalized with boastful vulgarity by the Nazi cinema and press, as well as in the very popular exhibit *The Soviet Paradise*, which was seen by more than a million visitors in 1942.

The Soviet slave was not free to work. He was forced to work by an inhuman regime that was the enemy of his people. In complete contrast, the German worker embodied and realized his freedom, since he was happy to contribute to the work of national rejuvenation. This refrain, repeated in every register, convinced no one, including the regime's hierarchs, who were not deceived by their own propaganda and who were very aware that in order to avoid a revolt or a revolution and not to end up like Wilhelm

II in 1918, they had to provide the Reich's workers with tangible satisfactions—that is, as the historian Götz Aly put it, they had to "buy the Germans."[59] That required a social and fiscal policy that was advantageous for "Germanic" subjects: lowering taxes and increasing welfare benefits—everything being financed by the spoliations imposed on the regime's political enemies and on Jews who had gone into exile, as well as by the predations of the war to come, which were greedily anticipated. The Reich depended fiscally, socially, and economically on credit to finance its war economy and to encourage the German worker to toil without grumbling too much.

In labor and economic life, as in everyday politics, the leaders of the Reich paid extremely close attention to the consent of the German people. Obtaining assent, and even participation, was their constant preoccupation, demonstrated right to the end: history, that of the revolutions of 1917 in Russia and 1918 in Germany, among others, proved that intelligence and repression were only marginally useful as complements to a vast policy aimed at unity. Confronted by the masses' discontent, a government never lasted long, even if it was as formidable as that of the czars in Russia or as rooted in society and culture as that of the Hohenzollern in Germany. In addition, since Bismarck, the French collapse of 1870, and the Paris Commune of 1871, this succession of defeat and revolution had frightened the powerful. A word to the wise sufficed: the continued existence of the government would not be ensured by a simple alliance between the truncheon and the microphone, between the watchtower and propaganda. More was required, much more, to involve and motivate a population to work, and then to fight and kill.

In the economic domain, it appeared immediately necessary to create management, a *Menschenführung*, that made promises and fulfilled them in order to motivate people and create a productive community.

It is here that National Socialism's tone, if not its sensibility, was revealed to be prodigiously useful. Hitler had never taken it seriously; moreover, he politically marginalized, and then physically eliminated, all those in the ranks of the NSDAP who sincerely believed in the project of a national socialism. Since its birth in Bavaria in 1919 to 1920, national *socialism* had been a political trap, a semantic delusion, that sought to attract all those who were tempted by socialist or communist internationalism to the nation. It remains that, for tactical reasons, this promise had been kept, particularly for the benefit of German workers. The film *Der Herrscher*, which shows the rise of a simple worker to the rank of magnate, thus reflected, at the level of the enterprise, the promise already kept at the political level by the advent of Adolf Hitler. The latter was constantly represented as the corporal who had risen through the ranks to become, through his gifts and his hard work, the head of a great nation. Similarly, old Clausen announced that the leadership of his enterprises would go to a worker who had emerged from the workshops, and who had distinguished himself by his remarkable and meritorious *Leistung*.

Thus, promotion is the culmination of effort: work will be rewarded by political power or by economic leadership. Since not everyone can become a supreme leader, this principle will be equally valid at every level, where big shots in uniform, foremen and little bosses proliferate. One of the Third Reich's mottoes is the famous phrase over the entrance of the Buchenwald concentration camp: "To each his due," or to each according to his merits (*Jedem das Seine*), a definition of justice by equity rather than by equality.[60] The break with the old regime, that of the *Kaiserreich*, is thus clear, at least verbally: it is no longer birth or relationships, heritage or social capital, that ensure advancement, but merit. The lessons taught by the missions of productivity conducted since the 1920s by German engineers in the United States had been learned well: the worker must not be driven to desperation, but, on the contrary, given things to dream about. Henry Ford—a Taylorist potentate without scruples, the great master of assembly-line production and the enslavement of bodies, an anti-Semitic essayist and a sincere admirer of the Third Reich—compensated for this inhuman alienation by holding out the prospect, not only of developing a potential career for everyone, but also of access to ownership (the workers who produced the Model T were supposed to drive it in the meantime).

In addition to this delightful prospect, that of a change in status, of promotion and social advancement, even socially and fiscally advantageous policies, German workers had also to be given a balm that eased their work, and helped them find pleasure or even "joy" in it. The model here was Italian and, more precisely, fascist. It was on the model of the Italian Dopolavoro that the organization Kraft durch Freude ("Strength through Joy") was created; it could be defined as an immense leisure organization spanning the Reich as a whole.

The idea was simple: productive power was sustained by joy, a joy produced by pleasure and leisure. As everywhere in the industrialized West, "leisure" had good press in the 1930s, which saw the French Front Populaire make it a political talking point, and even a governmental department. In Nazi Germany, leisure was meaningful solely in relation to work: it existed only to relax, rest, and reinvigorate workers by regenerating their ability to work—and it is for that reason that the KdF organization was incorporated into and subordinated to the German Labor Front (Deutsche Arbeitsfront, DAF), a corporatist organization and the sole union in the Third Reich, of which it was a subdivision. Kraft durch Freude supported the existence and the mission of the German Labor Front: as of May 2, 1933, the DAF replaced all syndicalist organizations, and its task was to organize German production in an optimal way. The single labor union, a corporatist organization, thus put an end to class struggle and to the sterile oppositions between managers and employees or workers. Its division entrusted with leisure activities, the KdF's mission was to make the workplace beautiful and happy, and to allow the reconstitution of the workers' productive strength. It was the KdF that organized classical music concerts in factories, kindly covered by the Reich's newsreels when a star of the artistic world, such as Herbert von Karajan, was the conductor. A department of the KdF, the Schönheit der Arbeit ("Beauty of Work") organization was assigned to think about the decoration, ergonomics, labor safety, and leisure activities on the production site. An astonishing Nazi modernity: it was not yet the era of Fußball, yoga lessons, or "chief happiness officers," but the principle and the spirit are certainly the same. Well-being, if not joy, given its role in efficiency and the conditions of optimal productivity, had to be supervised.

From 1933 to 1939—that is, before the war—200 million Reichsmarks (more than a billion present-day Euros) in public funds were spent to improve lighting, ventilation, and workers' nutrition, as well as to create cafeterias, common rooms, business libraries, and gaming and sporting competitions. More than sincere sympathy for the fate of workers, these measures reflected a firm will to increase their productivity. Creating rivalry and a competitive spirit was also on the agenda: businesses that rigorously applied the principles of the "Beauty of Work" department might be distinguished by the title of "National Socialist Model Enterprise" (*NS Musterbetrieb*).

Reassured by a transfigured workplace, the worker was also cared for outside the factory or the office. There again, the goal was to strengthen and reconstitute workers' productive power through leisure activities that would permit them to return to their job fully rested and ready to work. Thus, the KdF organization offered hikes, maritime cruises, and all-expenses paid vacations in purpose-built resorts in the mountains or at the seaside, such as the gigantic site of Prora, on the island of Rügen, with its six-kilometer-long hotel and its 20,000 beds. From 1933 to 1939, 36 million short trips and 7 million long trips and stays were organized, including 700,000 cruises on "KdF ships," liners constructed and outfitted by the organization itself. The "socialist" promise had its limits: the cruises were reserved for employees and managers because their cost (120 RM) was beyond the workers' means (their average monthly salary was 150 RM). Instead, workers could go on excursions in the mountains of Bavaria for a few days—at the time, this was not negligible—or go to the theater, the cinema, or museums (and there were almost 40 million visits made up until 1939).

In 1936, a KdF Olympic village was built to house tens of thousands of *Volksgenossen* who had come for the summer Olympic Games in Berlin—the sports spectacle being a source of competition that was supposed to be reflected, according to Hitler's own explicit wishes, in physical health, productive strength, and military aggressiveness.

The ultimate reward for the German worker was a "KdF car," the *KdF-Wagen* designed by Ferdinand Porsche. It was produced starting in 1938, and after 1945, it was known by the popular name of "Beetle." The *Volkswagen*, literally, "people's car," was one of the many promises not kept by the Third Reich. Its production was halted in 1939 in order to produce *Kübelwagen*, military vehicles similar to US Jeeps, in KdF factories built *ex nihilo* in Wolfsburg. But this promise had led more than 300,000 people to make subscription payments to KdF. The "people's car" was supposed to be the Reich's Model T: a motivation, a reward, and the spearhead of Germany's motorization.

Ergonomic improvements, common rooms, the organization of collective leisure activities . . . all these perks were reserved for members of the "community of the people," a community to be constructed and brought into existence, and not at all for racial aliens, the foreign workers who were flowing into the Reich from 1939 onwards. While the national territory was being emptied of its men, who were conscripted into the military, foreigners took their place, as volunteer or forced labor: the Third Reich, which wanted to rid its territory of all otherness, absorbed 15 million foreign workers before 1945. They were seen as a source of energy that could be exploited to the point of exhaustion in the case of Polish workers, workers from the East (*Ostarbeiter*), and detainees in concentration camps. Considered biologically as non-humans, they constituted, from an economic point of view, a subhuman or infra-human resource, to be treated as such. No management and no consideration: that was the only constraint, along with fierce repression of those foreign to the "community."

CHAPTER 5
FROM THE SS TO MANAGEMENT:
REINHARD HÖHN'S AKADEMIE FÜR FÜHRUNGSKRÄFTE

R eflections on the organization of labor, on the optimization of factors of production, and on the most efficient productive society were numerous and intense under the Third Reich not only because they responded to urgent if not vital questions, but also because there was an elite of young academics in Germany who liked to combine knowledge and action, scientific inquiry and technocracy. Several dozen of these found a natural place in the SS's intelligence service (the SD),[61] while the others were scattered throughout the myriad institutions and agencies created *ad hoc* under the Nazi government, that is, if they didn't simply take advantage of the windfall offered by the political and racial purge of the universities, which dismissed a third of their professors, assistants, and researchers, thus freeing up thousands of positions, from April 7, 1933 onwards.

Reinhard Höhn was, along with Werner Best, Wilhelm Stuckart, Otto Ohlendorf and so many others, the archetype of the technocratic intellectual. He was also, by dint of his radicality and his avant-garde ideas, as well as his reflections on the gradual disappearance of the state, the latter's most advanced spearhead.

It might be said that Höhn was a sort of Josef Mengele of the law, or in any case his counterpart. Whereas Mengele used his talents and exhausted his ambition by torturing twins, Höhn created and analyzed juridical concepts to regenerate the German community and reconfigure Europe, "community" and

Lebensraum being his two chief subjects of preoccupation and reflection before 1945.

Höhn was born in 1904, in Thuringia.[62] His father had risen in the juridical hierarchy by his own efforts, finally becoming an *Amtsanwalt*—a kind of adjunct prosecutor. Mengele was seven years younger than he. Mengele was Bavarian and came from a family of industrialists—today, the name of Mengele is still reputable in the domain of agricultural machinery. The two men were defined by their intellectual and social ambition. With their regular features, irreproachable haircuts, and cultivated manners, they were at ease in human intercourse and in society, holding a glass in their hand or attending a meeting at work, even if their books, their notebooks, or their lab benches remained their favorite refuge and the most reliable instrument of their insatiable will to power.

A relentless worker, Höhn was a student of the most conservative nationalist right wing, without, however, being a Nazi. He studied law and economics at the University of Kiel, then in Munich; he was a member of the Young German Order (Jungdeutscher Orden), an anti-Semitic and anti-communist group close to the NSDAP but opposed to Hitler's attempted putsch in 1923. Höhn left this group late, in January of 1932, after having been very active in it as a member, office holder, and theoretician. His ambition was to recreate, with the members of the order, a traditional German community seeking to avoid the dangers and errors of contemporary "society" and its individualism—a rather commonplace project at the time, and typical of the sensibility of the so-called "conservative revolution." He joined the NSDAP on May 1, 1933, and the SS in July; then he joined the SD, where he created and directed the *Lebensgebiete* department, whose mission was to study the different "life spaces" of the German people (universities, administrations, enterprises . . .), and to fight the enemies of the new government. In the meantime, Höhn had earned a doctor's degree in law, and in 1927, he defended his thesis in Jena (it was on a judge who dealt with criminal cases during the French Revolution).[63] In 1934, he received his *Habilitation* in Heidelberg, with a thesis in public law, *The Individualist Conception of the State and Its Legal Personhood*.[64] It was in Heidelberg that he had his first experience as a teacher, directing students pursuing independent studies. There, he probably taught the young law student Hanns Martin Schleyer,[65] a future SS captain in charge of the Aryanization of the Slovak economy, and after 1945, a CEO, before becoming head of the Confederation of German Employers' Associations and of the Federation of German Industries in the 1970s.

The "community" (*Gemeinschaft*) was Höhn's obsession; it was, in his view, the sole existing, normative reality. It is not the state that creates the people, but the community of the people that creates the state, which is a mere secondary instrument and in no case the supreme reality. Höhn insists all the more on this thesis because it is identical with that of the new masters, and of Hitler most of all, who saw the state as a reality subordinate to the *Volk* and the *Volksgemeinschaft*.

Höhn published numerous articles and essays on the "community" and on the reconfiguration of the great *Lebensraum* in the East, themes that were also dear to Carl Schmitt, whom Höhn courted and whom he sought, in the mid-1930s, to eliminate politically and academically. In 1936, when Schmitt's ambitions found expression in the major colloquium he organized on "Jewry in the Juridical Sciences,"[66] a series of articles appeared in the *Schwarzes Korps*, the SS's press organ, which were critical of the man who aspired to become the Third Reich's "crown lawyer." The basics were provided by Höhn,[67] who had made Himmler and Heydrich aware of the danger represented by Schmitt. The offense committed by Schmitt, who was a Catholic in love with Italy and France, was to be irremediably attached to the state, the principle and goal of juridical life. Too

Catholic, too Roman, too Latin, and too much a theologian, Schmitt, in domestic law, was a man of the state and not of race. In the domain of international law, the problem was at least as serious: in his writings, the East appears as a Great Space (*Großraum*) and not as a *Lebensraum*, a biotope. Too classical and too legalistic, too anchored in the traditional theory of international relations, his conception of spaces was not sufficiently biological. Schmitt thus appeared to be a man of the past, too timorous and mild in comparison with the Nazis' radical young lancers. He did all he could to be a perfect Nazi: he provided proofs of his nationalism and his obsessional anti-Semitism—which he never renounced, quite the contrary—but he was outflanked on his right by people more radical, more coherent, and more ambitious than he was.

Höhn was one of the SD's most promising managers: his inexhaustible intellectual energy, his plotting skills, and his worldly aptitudes made him a senior SS official and a first-rate schemer. Although he was liked and protected by Himmler and Heydrich, he nonetheless had many enemies who were able to exhume the most compromising quotations from his past in the "German Youth" movement: his speeches and articles were re-read by his opponents, who found in them ferocious criticisms of the NSDAP and Hitler. He was expelled from the SD leadership (his department was entrusted to Professor Six), and appointed to a professorship at the University of Berlin and became director of the Institute for State Research (Institut für Staatsforschung) housed in the SS's offices in Wannsee. The mission of this institute was to provide food for thought for the NSDAP, the ministry of Foreign Affairs, and the Wehrmacht regarding the best way to adapt state institutions to the future Great Reich. What structures and what reforms should be envisioned? Höhn pursued his theoretical work on the state, the community, and the agencies, and he created colloquia and publications on comparative administrative law. It was also in this context that he edited the publication of *Reich, Volksordnung, Lebensraum*, a review we have already discussed.

Höhn's work was so satisfactory that despite the plots directed against him, and thanks to Himmler's protection, he was able to pursue his career in the SS: promoted to the rank of *Standartenführer* (colonel) in 1939, he was made an *Oberführer* (general) in 1944 and finished the war at that rank.

For Höhn, as for his comrades, the year 1945 was a political catastrophe and a major biographical turning point. He had to reinvent himself by changing his location, his career, and his life. Each of the former SS officials found a different way to escape, but Reinhard Höhn did not; he stayed in Germany. Mengele hid in the mountains, then fled to Latin America, repeatedly changing his name. Other colleagues of Höhn's expended a wealth of energy and inventiveness to mask themselves and slip away. For instance, Hans Schneider, who held a doctorate in literature and was a captain in the SS and a member of the Ahnenerbe, disappeared without a trace; his wife declared that he was "missing" (*vermisst*), having died in combat or in the bombardments that hammered Germany in 1945. Schneider procured a false identity, that of a man who was really missing, and literally *remade* his life. He remade everything: he wrote another doctoral thesis, even though he already held a doctorate; he remarried his wife, who was now a fictive war widow; he continued on his way, was recertified as a teacher and became a university professor. Professor Hans Schwerte, a well-known specialist in contemporary German literature and rector of the Technical University of Aachen, was not unmasked until 1995.

Höhn didn't bother with any of these precautions. He did not flee to another continent or change his identity, except during a period of five years when he prudently had former SD colleagues forge papers in the name of "Rudolf Haeberlein," or "Uncle Rudy," as his two daughters called him. Höhn did not resume his real patronym until 1950. Like Klaus Barbie and many others, Professor Dr. Höhn succeeded in switching back to his former identity by not changing a thing: after the war, he became what he had always been. It was the Nazis who, unlike Eichmann or Mengele, wanted to change everything—their careers, their lives—who failed.

When the Reich collapsed, Höhn initially found himself without a job, rank, or social status. The unconditional surrender destroyed his places of socialization and employment: the SS and the SD disappeared, as did his teaching position at the University of Berlin, where he held a chair by virtue of his functions in the SD and Heinrich Himmler's insistence. In the general chaos, Höhn disappeared and evaded any prosecution on the part of the Allies or in the German courts: not having personally commanded a unit of killers on the Eastern front, he was not one of the chief targets. It was a hard time. Höhn-Haeberlein established himself in Lippstadt, a small town in Westphalia, as a *Heilpraktiker* (paramedical practioner), a status that is still regulated in Germany by a law passed in 1939 that covers all therapists practicing unconventional forms of medical care. Höhn, who had had a keen interest in Buddhism since he was a teenager, had been trained in the laying on of hands by his landlady in Lippstadt, who was fond of Tarot and practiced acupuncture and homeopathy. He was questioned by the police because he had placed a plaque on his office door with his title of *Professor Doktor*, omitting to mention that he was a doctor and professor of law, not of medicine. For this white lie, a venial sin, he was judged guilty and was forced to pay a fine and cease his activity. This was his only trouble with the law in the immediate postwar period until, in 1958, a tribunal in Berlin sentenced him to pay a fine of 12,000 DM for having spread Nazi ideas to students when he was a professor under the Third Reich:[68] 12,000 DM, or about 1,500 present-day Euros, to settle everything. It would seem fair to say that he got off pretty cheaply.

After this interlude as a naturopath, Höhn's situation rapidly improved, thanks to the networks of solidarity that connected the approximately 6,500 alumni of the SD (out of 50,000 people who had been employed by the RSHA—the Reichssicherheitshauptamt, the headquarters of the Reich's security service). These networks were active and powerful, with former SS technocrats and intellectuals found throughout the world of administration, universities, the judicial system, and the economy. The former managers of the Great Reich were particularly popular in the private sector, where their excellent training (usually as lawyers) and their experience at the head of the Reich's organizations were prized, and where people remembered the excellent business deals that had been made over the past twelve years thanks to rearmament and the profitable cooperation between German industry and the SS's concentration camp empire. Thus, after the foundation of the Bundesrepublik Deutschland (BRD; Federal Republic of Germany, FRG), a "National-Socialist penetration of the BRD"[69] worked to the advantage of former criminals, who escaped any problems in the courts or saw their sentences commuted and reduced.

Thus, Höhn benefited from the help and advice of Ernst Aschenbach, who held a doctorate in law and was also a diplomat, the former head of the political office in the Reich's embassy in France and, in this capacity, involved in the deportation of Jews from France to Germany. Having become a lawyer in Essen, Dr. Aschenbach very actively supported Nazi criminals in court, but also in the halls of power in Bonn, where he was a presence because of his terms of office as a federal representative for the FDP (Free Democratic Party). It was Aschenbach (a close associate of Werner Best, who was also involved in defending his "old comrades") who guided Höhn along the paths of legal rehabilitation. The amnesty law of December 31, 1949 wiped clean Höhn's slate, along with those of 800,000 other Nazis. But the SS networks did not limit themselves to providing

papers, good conduct certificates, and penal virginity. SS solidarity also enabled positions and jobs for "veterans," with
alumni found in groups with political and economic power,
even those close to Adenauer, within the chancellery and at the
heart of the administrative councils and the general leadership
of the largest enterprises.

Some became business lawyers, members of boards of directors, managers, and directors of institutions, while others, like
Höhn, remained loyal to their intellectual and pedagogic vocations.

In the early 1950s, Höhn was invited to give lectures on
military history in the context of strategic thought by an old
acquaintance, General Heinrich Eberbach (the former commander in chief of the *Panzergruppe West*, and then of the
Eighth Army, before he became the administrator of the Evan-
gelical Academy, a respected Protestant think tank). The Bonn
government was beginning to consider the possibility of recon-
stituting a German army: confronted by the Soviet enemy, it was
desirable not only to rearm economically through the Marshall
Plan and the ECSC (European Coal and Steel Community), but
also to rearm, period. Despite the unspeakable disasters of the
war and the first projects for the complete and eternal disar-
mament of Germany, the ECSC even considered establishing
a European Defense Community (EDC), of which the German
enemy, having conveniently become a friend, would be a full-
fledged member. Known for his work on military history after
publishing his voluminous *Revolution, Heer, Kriegsbild* in 1944,
Höhn was one of the experts who helped create the military
tool of today and tomorrow. He eagerly seized the opportunity,
cultivating and expanding the network that his past in the SS
provided him. He also enjoyed clear advantages in comparison to his former comrades: his academic skills, his immense
culture and his ability to problematize, expound, and write, as
well as his talents as an orator and a teacher, his inexhaustible
energy and his capacity for work—all this immediately singled

him out as having great potential that could be exploited. That was, moreover, exactly what he needed to reconstruct a social standing he was worthy of and to find an occupation suited to his talents and ambitions. This did not escape the notice of senior directors of German business enterprises.

In 1953, we thus find Höhn in the position of director of the German Society for Political Economy (Deutsche Volkswirtschaftliche Gesellschaft, DVG), an association and industrial think tank that sought, in the context of a high growth rate, to promote the most efficient management methods. In order to "develop and teach the forms of human resources management best suited to [its] time,"[70] the DVG decided to create a business school for the managers of the economy. In the context of the Marshall Plan, triumphant Atlanticism, and "productivity missions" in the United States, the goal was to train managers like those in America, versatile leaders distinct from the specialists, the doctors of this or engineers of that, of whom Germany had been so fond since the reign of Wilhelm II. The model was, obviously, Harvard Business School, which was to be duplicated in Germany as it was in France with the creation of INSEAD (Institut Européen d'Administration des Affaires) in 1957.

The foundation of the elite German school of management was concomitant to that of INSEAD. In 1956, the DVG proudly opened a campus in the charming and picturesque city of Bad Harzburg, located in the foothills of the Harz Mountains in Lower Saxony. In that year, one year after the Bundesrepublik founded its army, the Bundeswehr, and saw the end of ten years of Allied occupation, the Management Academy (Akademie für Führungskräfte) was opened in Bad Harzburg under the direction of the man who, eleven years earlier, was still "SS-Oberführer Professor Dr. Reinhard Höhn." By the time its founder died in 2000, this school had trained some 600,000 managers from the main German companies, not to mention the 100,000 who registered for distance learning.

Höhn rejoiced to be teaching there, as did other former members of the SS and the SD. Justus Beyer, who was born in 1910 and held a doctorate in law, had worked until 1941 on plans for the conquest and colonization of *Lebensraum* in the East, later became a member of the Nazi party chancellery, and was promoted, in June 1944, to the rank of *Obersturmbann-führer*. He taught at the Academy in the 1970s after teaching commercial law in an engineering school.

Another of Höhn's former colleagues in the SS became one of the pillars of the school in Bad Harzburg: Professor Franz Alfred Six, a friend and protector of Beyer. Six, born in 1909, had pursued a rapid and brilliant university career in a discipline that was still young, "Newspaper Sciences" (*Zeitungswissenschaften*), which focused on journalism and drew on the various human and social sciences. He received a doctorate at the age of twenty-five, with a thesis defended in Heidelberg on *The Political Propaganda of National Socialism* (1934), and earned his *Habilitation* three years later with a study on *The Press of National Minorities in the German Reich*. In the same year, he was appointed University Professor in Königsberg, at the improbable age of twenty-eight, joining the faculty of the University of Berlin in 1940. At the same time, his career grew just as quickly within the SD and the SS, for which he served as the press expert starting in 1935, and then succeeded his colleague and comrade Höhn as head of the department assigned to do "research on opponents" (*Gegnerforschung—Amt* II) in 1939, and "ideological research" (*Weltanschauliche Forschung—Amt* VII) in 1942. In 1941, he was given command of an SS unit and of the German police in Russia, attached to the SS General Arthur Nebe's *Einsatzgruppe* B. This experience in the field made him guilty of war crimes and of crimes against humanity, as his biographer Lutz Hachmeister has clearly shown.[71] Tried in Nuremberg during the "*Einsatzgruppen* trial," he was sentenced in 1948 to twenty years in prison, but he was released in 1952. The support of former SS men like Werner Best allowed him to become an important editor who worked for the center-left weekly *Der Spiegel*, and he was also a member of the conservative and economically liberal FDP, which regularly whitewashed former Nazis. In 1957, he became the advertising director for the Porsche company, and then an independent consultant in 1963. On the side, the former *Brigadeführer* Six taught marketing at the Academy in Bad Harzburg. In 1968, the school's press published his marketing manual, which collected together the substance of his teaching,[72] and which, because of its success, was reprinted in 1971.

The students trained at the *Akademie* were practitioners, people who were already managers and had been sent there by their employers for a few weeks or months of further training. A top school of continuing education, it was comparable to its French counterpart, INSEAD, or to any business school producing MBAs to serve as managers. Both the cream and the drudges of the "German economic miracle" attended the seminars directed by Reinhard Höhn and his colleagues: managers from Aldi, BMW, Hoechst, but also Bayer, Telefunken, Esso, Krupp, Thyssen, and Opel, not to forget Ford, Colgate, Hewlett-Packard, and even the reigning queen of sex-shops and porn, Beate Uhse International which, like 2,500 other companies, sent its managers to listen to the lessons taught by former SS officers. The Bundeswehr was also among the clients of this business school, because, like anyone who scorned the state, Höhn did not refuse its subsidies when it offered them. Höhn's work on military history interested German commanders, and the "delegation of responsibility" he advocated corresponded in spirit to the ethos of the new German officer and the culture of the new army, which was steeped in *innere Führung* ("autonomous conduct") for its "citizens in uniform," who were free even in rank and file. Höhn succeeded in remaking himself.

A captivating lecturer, a professor who impressed these private managers who were fascinated by his rhetoric, his culture, and his humor, Höhn had everything necessary to establish himself in an economic and managerial milieu where great minds were not in the majority. In the second half of the 1950s, he regained a monthly income and living conditions comparable to those he had enjoyed in 1942–43, at the peak of his Nazi career. In 1956, he was earning 2,000 DM a month, or the equivalent of about 5,000 Euros today, not counting royalties on his books and various fees. To celebrate this newly recovered prosperity, he bought a green Mercedes like the one he had in the 1940s—green like his taste for nature and like the jacket he wore for hunting, a pastime in which he engaged passionately. The Mercedes was affectionately nicknamed, as in 1942, "Little Frog" (*Laubfrosch*), in a family in which everyone seemed to love one another tenderly. Höhn, whose charisma was pleasing, despite his propensity for talking too much and too fast, was not loath to have affairs here and there, but he remained a *Familienmensch* and a loving father for his two daughters born in the late 1930s. He had taken great pains to make sure they were safe, having evacuated them from Berlin very early on so they would escape the bombardments. From Thuringia, where they took refuge with family, they marvelled at the success of their father, who worked hard and gradually became the manager-in-chief of the Federal Republic of Germany.

CHAPTER 6
THE ART OF (ECONOMIC) WAR

Military history was the passion of Reinhard Höhn the lawyer, an indefatigable polygraph and hard worker. He appears to have devoted his evenings and weekends to his hobby, with intense ruminations which resulted in several hefty volumes. Höhn's abundant bibliography—as lawyer, manager and amateur historian—thus includes three works on military history. One of these seems central, from a conceptual as well as a personal point of view. I refer to the study he devoted to *Scharnhorst's Legacy* (*Scharnhorsts Vermächtnis*),[73] which he published in 1952, at a time when the political elites of the young Bundesrepublik, in the middle of the Cold War, were intensely considering, with the blessing of the Western powers, the creation of a new German army. This work of reflection and reorganization led to the foundation, in 1955, of the Bundeswehr, a federal army closely associated with the West and with the democratic and individualistic principles of the new Germany. With his essay on Gerhard von Scharnhorst, a famous reformer of the Prussian army in the dark years between 1806 and 1813, Höhn announced, if not his candidacy, at least his presence in the debates and reflections of this crucial period. His book, in offering an intellectual biography of a reformer, posits a scarcely veiled analogy between one period of defeat (Prussia crushed by Napoleon at Jena and Auerstedt) and another (the collapse in 1945). It also suggests another: the great Scharnhorst being succeeded by other, more contemporary reformers—and in particular Höhn himself. The ideas proposed here are, moreover, just as valid for economic war: Höhn's extreme attention to the reform of the *managers* of the army is also addressed to the managers of business enterprises—those modern armies. Also striking is the continuity between the ideas, themes, and obsessions of the 1930s and 1940s and those that govern Höhn's historical and managerial work from the 1950s to the 1990s. There is no discontinuity, no break, in his fundamental intuitions, his postulates, and his principles—apart from in his obsession with race, the Jewish peril, and the conquest of the great *Lebensraum*.

The first principle is the attention given to practice: in this case, to military history. In the 1930s, Höhn the lawyer had already distinguished himself through his interest in sociology, which he taught as a seminar leader, and in history. The *mise en abyme* is flattering: like Clausewitz, Scharnhorst was a devotee of history and practice. Nazi jurists, including Höhn, never ceased to call for an examination of the "real," of "individual cases," praising "case law" (*Fallrecht*) and oral custom, exalting "concrete orders" and sanctifying personal intuition, the "people's common sense," in opposition to any abstraction, codification, or bookish learning. Höhn's essay on Scharnhorst vigorously condemns "military positivism,"[74] just as juridical positivism had been stigmatized by Höhn and his colleagues, who saw in it a Jewish mania.

Abstraction is the rule. The rule is dogma, and dogma is death. Without deviating from the intellectual course of his Nazi years, Höhn exalts life and concrete experience over the geometrical, mathematical temptation to formulate rules applicable to every case. Take Frederick II of Prussia: his genius lay precisely in the fact that in every case, he knew how to adapt himself to the conditions he encountered; life is nothing other than plasticity, flexibility, adaptability. What does not change, does not adapt, disappears, like every species that is no longer adapted to survive in a given environment. In other words, the Prussian army perished in 1806 because it had adopted

Frederick II and his tactical principles as intangible, atemporal norms of the art of war. What had been life, spontaneity, and perpetual adaptation—in short, the "elasticity" (that term again!) of every instant—was mummified. "It seems that Frederick the Great was not the great general par excellence, but only a great general. He was in no way dogmatic and infallible, he was not the patron saint of the art of war."[75] The same holds for Napoleon, who was not the inventor of a "system":[76] "The genius we admire in them resides in something very different. Their 'great spirit,' Scharnhorst wrote, 'did not follow rules, but found in the circumstances themselves the most favorable measures for each particular case.'"[77] Frederick II became "the idol of positivist soldiers,"[78] whereas it is "absurd to want to find dogmas in general recommendations that must always be adapted to situations, as the king himself did."[79]

Against the petrification of thought, the goal must be to recover the taste and energy of innovation: "combatting military positivism"[80] requires us to rid ourselves of "tradition"[81] when the latter is no longer "adapted to the new times."[82]

Abstraction, combined with an unjustified worship of the authorities of the past, leads to great catastrophes like that of 1806. Frederick II's successes elevated his "linear tactics" into an apodictic truth that had been taught since the Seven Years' War by generations of generals with the fervor of the faithful follower and the rigor of the geometrician. The result was that "the army was reduced to a machine whose internal workings had become an object of worship, while the art of war had become a system of mathematical calculation."[83] Now, everything is merely "mechanism," "mechanical" and "mathematical,"[84] "mathematical formulas and mechanical rules."[85] The army is manipulated and maneuvered like "a dead figure," so "crushing [is] the weight of this positivist system."[86]

In these pages, as throughout Höhn's military writings, we find an almost overt indictment of the Nazi art of war, the one that led, in 1945, to a defeat still graver than that of 1806. In the end, the Third Reich was too mechanistic, too abstract, and too authoritarian, contrary to the principles that lawyers, thinkers, and enlightened managers like Höhn and his colleagues formulated in one article after another: divisions were moved around like pawns, illusory lines were erected, and human masses were played with on *Kriegspiel* maps. The same methods were applied on different terrains, and the Blitzkrieg was paralyzed by "orders to halt" that froze movement and multiplied battles that slowed down the army's advance. In addition, the *Volksgenossen*, in their economic production as in their military duties, were not sufficiently involved or motivated. The Wehrmacht's non-commissioned officers were as rigid, authoritarian, and stupid as their predecessors in 1806, who saw in the soldier simply a cog in a machine.

In diametrical opposition to this mechanistic conception of military action—which postulates that an unhindered concatenation between the strategic plan, the particular order, and its execution is the guarantee of victory—the French invented, during the Revolution, a new art of war based on personal motivation and the involvement of everyone, as well as on a surprising flexibility of execution, which guaranteed tactical agility and success.

Starting in 1792, Höhn notes, the French no longer fought for a cabinet, a minister, or a king, but very concretely, for themselves, for the form they wanted to give to their lives: "In mass conscription," he said, "it is the people (*das Volk*) as a whole that are mobilized," and each of these people is fighting "for political ideals"[87] that are very concrete. It is in and by combat that "the subject becomes a citizen."[88] French combatants were moved by "enthusiasm,"[89] an "enthusiasm that was the fanatical will to impose the Revolution"[90]—the expression *fanatischer Wille* being a very common Nazi phrase like many others found in Höhn's work; the deep rhetorical geology survived the collapse of 1945. As evidence of this, among many examples, is the following phrase: the enthusiasm of the French "was expressed militarily by a disposition toward sacrifice that was prepared to go to any lengths and to use all possible means"[91]—a phrase that seems to have been taken directly from one of the many diehard tracts that the Nazis published in 1945. The German armed forces, Höhn argued, had not been able fully to deploy these ideals and virtues exalted by the Third Reich because they had not gone far enough in "German liberty," in the liberation of the individual and his potential for aggression and action. Instead of liberating energies, they constrained and repressed them: "the soldier remained a number. It was through constraint that he had been trained for purely mechanical battles. The moral bond, people said, was created by the corporal's stick," through physical punishment. The French, in contrast, staked everything on "the liberation of the individual from an absolutist constraint."[92]

The wars of the Revolution and the Empire, waged between 1792 and 1815, pitted "the strength of a people against traditional armies"[93] fossilized in their obsolete certainties. From a tactical point of view, Höhn goes on, this confrontation pitted the rigid battle lines, inherited from the Seven Years' War thirty or forty years earlier, against the mobile, quick, fluid "skirmishers" who sowed despair in the ranks of a Prussian army corseted by discipline in the stupidest kinds of drills.

However, the goal was not to make the skirmisher the new alpha and omega of the art of war, but rather to grasp his spirit, which is what Napoleon did with the greatest aptness and effectiveness. The skirmisher, a mobile, dynamic, and free combatant, was, from a tactical point of view, adapted to the most difficult terrains, whereas a line of riflemen remained useful on an open battlefield. Thus, the point was not to become dogmatic in the opposite direction, but to move beyond the opposition between skirmishers and lines by combining the two:

"The elasticity of the method of combat that characterizes the skirmisher system must be extended to the army as a whole."[94] In practice, the goal was to raise "the profound meaning" of the "skirmisher system" from tactics to strategy: "The opposition between line and skirmisher disappears [. . .] and a new unity appears when the spirit of war as a whole is guided by the principles of the skirmisher system."[95] Thus, the goal was not to dogmatically abolish lines of foot soldiers but to make them as mobile, agile, and flexible as the new combatants introduced by the Revolutionary armies: there will be fixed lines if necessary, and they will move if necessary. Napoleon had well understood this "elasticity" and made it a lever of his success. Following his example, "we must conduct battles in accord with the deep principle of skirmishers' combat,"[96] in order to "make the rigid system that formerly prevailed more flexible."[97]

This rigidity concerned soldiers most of all, in the physical sense as well. Höhn seems to have been very preoccupied with the soldier, and insisted over and over in his writings that the day of the soldier-machine was past: "The soldier himself can no longer be considered a simple machine for marching and firing his weapon [. . .]. The corporal punishments that had, up to that time, been considered necessary for 'training' him became useless,"[98] as was proven by the spontaneous enthusiasm, motivation, and commitment of the French volunteers in the Revolution's armies. However, Höhn does not linger on the revolutionary autonomy of the soldier-citizen: he notes that the latter were fighting for themselves, their ideas, and their freedom, but he does not transpose this model to the Prussian soldier, because Scharnhorst does not do so, either.

What interested Scharnhorst, and what interested Höhn in the work of the great Prussian reformer, was less the rank-and-file soldier, the basic combatant, than corps of officers and non-commissioned officers—in other words, the managers: "For Scharnhorst, the culmination of the work of progress was the systematic re-education of the officer corps,"[99] which had to learn to "think"[100] (*denken*). The word *denken* should probably be translated here as "consider": the point is less to conceive the ends than to consider the means of attaining the objectives defined by the high command. Thus, for Scharnhorst and Höhn, "thinking" does not mean lofty contemplation but rather aptitude for the most basic reflection. It is not a matter of reflecting on the objectives and critiquing them, but rather of being able to realize them by means of an optimal adaptation to combat on the battlefield: "An officer who thinks considers in a critical way all military dogmas as well as all new military ideologies: he evaluates their utility in practical implementation"[101] and must "use his capacity of judgment in action."[102] In this context, *denken* hence means less "conceiving" (the ends) than "calculating" (the means).

In opposition to aristocratic officers' "traditional hostility to any training" and to their predilection for "routine, inherited from one generation to the next by drilling,"[103] Höhn sought to create a military "academy"[104] to train managers in the practice of economic war. This training was to be resolutely practical, and not theoretical. Like Scharnhorst and Napoleon themselves, the young managers had to be nourished by military history and case studies,[105] and avoid abstractions "foreign to war."[106] The army's managers had to be neither trained monkeys nor academics stuffed with knowledge. They should have nothing more than what was strictly necessary to know how and be able to maneuver and triumph: their baggage had to be minimal and unencumbered by a scholasticism cultivated like art for art's sake. Mathematics, once so prized, was reduced to profit-loss calculus and the geometry necessary for reading maps and understanding maneuvers.[107]

These efforts and this reform of military understanding were necessary for a "new generation without prejudices, oriented toward practice, and trained for personal reflection" through the possession "of an elementary knowledge of tactics."[108]

Scharnhorst, Höhn enthuses, saw his projects culminated in the opening of a "young officer's academy," of which he became director;[109] Höhn himself held the ambition, in the early 1950s, to direct an academy for corporate managers. Protected from "theories foreign to life" and aware of the reality of the terrain, trained "for applied tactics and strategy,"[110] these officers would, in the future, show that they were capable of "practicing elastic combat,"[111] like Napoleon, who had been able to form mobile, rapid, flexible divisions, each with its own staff, acting almost like a skirmisher.[112]

The new "elastic strategy"[113]—that is, a flexible and adaptative strategy—was, therefore, less about the soldier than his officer or non-commissioned officer who had been trained for flexible practice and adapted to the situation in each case. What was most important was "a sharp eye, seeing the essential elements" of "each particular case"[114] and of the terrain: "The officer and non-commissioned officer are thus freed from the hindrances imposed by rigid orders. His ability to make his own decisions is now given a broad scope. He has to find by himself the means and the avenues that lead to the objective defined by the task that has been assigned to him."[115] Everything is said here, in the most explicit and clear manner: the officer in the field, like the manager, in no way participates in the definition of the objective, because the latter has been assigned to him within the limits of a task to be accomplished. It is not for him to decide which hill to take or which destination to reach, or to repudiate that objective as completely absurd. His sole freedom is to find, by himself, autonomously, the way to achieve the objective. He is, therefore, free to obey.

This association of an authoritarian command, incontestable and uncontested in its supreme prerogatives, with the freedom granted to officers in the field was called by Scharnhorst and his reform-minded colleagues "mission-type tactics,"

Auftragstaktik. A mission is given to the officer or non-commissioned officer: he is then free to carry it out using whatever means he chooses. He is, therefore, free to obey and to succeed. Centralizing rigidity in the definition of objectives and strategy by the high command—and allowing flexibility in the execution in the field: this method bore fruit, to judge by the impressive series of victories won by the Prussian army against the French (1813–15), German revolutionaries (1849), the Danish (1864), the Austrians (1866) and again the French (1870–71). The Prussian non-commissioned officer won his stripes as a legendary figure while, at the same time, bearing the weight of potential failure on his shoulders and subjecting his subordinates, ordinary foot soldiers, to all its pressure. Glorified by the merit of his victories, the Prussian officer or non-commissioned officer remained, in both military practice and the collective imagination, the incarnation of the beetle-browed tyrant, the persnickety leader full of himself, the harrier without a soul. His strident violence and hob-nailed brutality became a commonplace of popular culture, in literature and, later, in film. Was this violence the natural prerogative, the necessary component of his ethos as a vociferous sergeant-instructor, or was it the possible expression of a terrible fear—that of failing when he was free to obey and obligated to win? On the shoulders of the field officer or the non-commissioned officer fell, heavy and harsh, the cascade of responsibilities and scorn proceeding from on high, from the Olympus where cadets and graduates of the war college conferred and conversed in staff meetings that defined, with complete freedom this time, the supreme objectives. At the lowest level, where there were no epaulets or shiny lanyards, no prestige or advantages due to rank, there remained only the crushing awareness of one's own responsibility. This system of command—of military management—theorized by Scharnhorst and the reformers and glorified by Höhn, thus proved to be remarkably efficacious and perverse. It was efficacious at least until World War I, and it was certainly also perverse then as well: the eminently contradictory injunction that weighed on management in the field was to be free without being in any way free. The corollary of this was, for the officer and the non-commissioned officer in the field, total and absolute responsibility, without having made any of the decisions.

As we have seen, Reinhard Höhn, though a lawyer, loved history and wanted to remain attentive to the "real" and the "concrete." In Prussian reformers of the years 1806–13, such as Scharnhorst, Gneisenau, and Clausewitz, he admired the ability to adapt and the flexibility that allowed them to put themselves in tune with the new era initiated by the French Revolution. The advent of the age of the masses and the individual, of the "nation" as opposed to traditional monarchies, had not escaped the attention of these sagacious minds.

In 1945, a defeat far more crushing and traumatizing than that of 1806 demanded that there be another reform. But calling for reform does not mean destroying and abandoning the past in its totality; quite the contrary. After 1806, people like Scharnhorst remained old-fashioned Prussian officers, steeped in a sense of "duty" and loyalty to their king. Similarly, Höhn did not disown all of his Nazi past. He gave up the rabid racism of the 1930s, anti-Semitism, and the quest for *Lebensraum*, but did not renounce certain fundamental lines of thought that he had developed—in his books and articles—in tandem with his colleagues. As he saw it, the Third Reich doubtless failed because it was not Nazi enough and had not sufficiently put into practice "German freedom"; that is, the flexibility and "elasticity" of its agents and agencies.

After 1945, and still more since the creation of the Federal Republic of Germany (Bundesrepublik Deutschland, BRD) in 1949, it was exactly the right time for freedom—that of the masses and that of the individual. A federal, democratic constitution had created a new state that saw itself as an outpost of democracy, opposing the Eastern Bloc. The BRD was in the vanguard of the "Free World" against the eternal communist enemy, which the Reich had already fought. Like tens of thousands of representatives of the old "Hitler elites"[116]—academics, journalists, CEOs, jurists, physicians, policemen, military men, etc.—Höhn was going to conscientiously put himself in the service of the new ideals of the time: the economic growth of the eponymous "miracle" and the triumph of Western freedom.

In an entirely opportune way, the conceptions of command and management Höhn and his colleagues had developed in the 1930s proved to be astonishingly in line with the spirit of the new era. After 1945, the lessons of history were established even more firmly than they had been earlier: leadership would have to change. That held for the army and for business enterprises, and even for the administration, in which the insatiable Höhn also took an interest.

In the army that was to be born in 1955, the Bundeswehr, the ideal of the "citizen in uniform" was established. In opposition to the "zombie-like obedience" advocated by the head of the SS, Heinrich Himmler, which was clearly very unfaithful to the precepts of German freedom, and against the mechanical discipline of a Wehrmacht that had forgotten Scharnhorst's lessons, it was necessary to institute a reflective obedience that could lead, at least in theory, to a refusal to obey illegitimate orders.

In business, however, this theory wouldn't be employed to its fullest. Höhn's great contribution was a model of management that seemed to be an appropriate expression of the new democratic culture—"management by delegation of responsibility."

For decades, this method of management, called the "Bad Harzburg Method," was the pride of the BRD. Professor Höhn's reflections represented the sole German or Germanic alternative to the prestigious authority of the Frenchman Henri Rayol or the American Peter Drucker, until the St. Gallen method, developed in Alemannic Switzerland, came to prominence in the early 1970s. Widely approved in Germany and in the Germanophone world, The Bad Harzburg method, its spirit, widespread influence and appropriation, make it possible to reconstruct a whole "German history of labor after 1945,"[117] in which the continuities with the Nazi period are very clear.

An indefatigable pedagogue and compulsive writer, Höhn set forth the principles of this history in the impressive series of works that he published, amended, and republished between 1956 and 1995—there are some forty of them out of the fifty works he published over the course of his life. This managerial literature proves to be as descriptive and normative as it is short on ideas. The sharp difference from the style and tone of his prewar publications is clear: whereas, before 1945, Höhn could still take pleasure in putting his legal analyses in their historical and cultural context, his textbooks written after 1956 are terribly dry: in them, schemas abound, as do case studies. In reality, Höhn was putting his lectures on paper and vice versa. These lectures were addressed to practitioners, to managers who were in a hurry to get back to running their units, and who had little desire to listen to discussions of the history of administration in the absolutist era. A true pedagogue, Höhn did not hesitate to respond to this demand for ready-to-consume wisdom. Moreover, the big textbooks are summed up in *compendia*, small books that present the essential points, published by the *Akademie*'s press. These sold, in multiple reprintings, hundreds of thousands of copies, like the best-seller entitled *The Daily Bread of Management*.[118] Nothing that has to do with management escapes his pen: neither *The Secretary and Her Boss*[119] nor *The Leadership of a Corporation*[120] (republished in 1995), as well as many other manuals and case studies on the board of directors or on management during an economic crisis, the latter being published opportunely in 1974.[121] Personal development also interested him, as is shown by his *Techniques of Intellectual Work: Overcoming Routine, Increasing Creativity*[122] reprinted in 1985. The manager also manages himself. Thus, coaching has an important place in the Akademie der Führungskräfte, because *Menschenführung* presupposes good *Lebensführung*. Hence, in order to "manage one's life" (a monstrous but fitting equivalent of *Leben führen*), and to cope better with one's "stress" and one's workload, managers were invited to attend Professor Dr. Karl Kötschau's seminars. This physician offered modules on dietetics, relaxation, maintenance, and athletics. A member of the NSDAP and the SA, Professor Kötschau had chosen "The National Socialist Idea in Biological Medicine" as the topic of his inaugural lecture at Jena (where he created the chair of "medical biology"). An advocate of the "Nazi revolution in medicine," Kötschau was a radical eugenicist firmly opposed to socialized health insurance and a prophet of the German man regenerated by the new medicine, freed of his sentimental, old-fashioned humanism: "The National Socialist hero is the man who enjoys his full biological and racial value," wrote this physician who was fond of homeopathy and who, after 1945, pursued the fight against *Fürsorge* (welfare support) in the name of *Vorsorge* (prevention, prophylaxis). As the director of a sanatorium in Bad Harzburg, he complemented his comfortable remuneration by talking about grated carrots and naturopathy with managers in search of a healthy lifestyle.

In his many writings, Höhn presented his modern management style as the expression of an era. The age of absolutism or dictatorship was over. In the age of the democratic masses, every individual wanted to be respected for who he was not as a "subordinate," but as a "co-worker," "a person who thinks and acts autonomously":[123] "People must be directed differently [. . .] The mutations in our economic, technical, and sociological environment are giving rise to a new style of direction."[124]

Working with "co-workers" responds to one of Höhn's deepest concerns: the need to eliminate class struggle from economic society as well as from political society. The new hierarchical relationship averts the risk of a confrontation between the dominators and the dominated, between bosses and employees. In 1942, Höhn used these terms to salute one of the great merits of the Nazi community: "Instead of the relation between the state and the subject, we have the community of the people," which is based on "the fundamental laws of life, race, and soil," and implies "the integration of the worker into the community of production and performance [*Leistungsgemeinschaft*] of the people as a whole."[125] The grand plan of the Nazi community having been swept away by the defeat of 1945, it remained possible to cultivate communitarian harmony between "leadership" (*Führung*) and "personnel" (*Gefolgschaft*)[126] within the "community of production and performance" represented by the business enterprise. Peaceful social relationships would allow optimized production as well as the strengthening of a West German society confronted by the great ideological, economic, and geostrategic enemy—the Eastern Bloc and its competing economic system, "socialism," beginning with East Germany's "real socialism."

What the *Betriebsgemeinschaft* (community of workers and bosses in a business enterprise) was under the Third Reich, Höhn sought to continue with his project—a community of managers and their free co-workers—in the democratic universe of West Germany, with its ordoliberal and participative "social market economy" in which, following a law passed in 1951 by the Christian Democrats and the Christian Social Union, cooperative management and decision-making (*Mitbestimmung*) were supposed to reign. On the level of the economy as a whole, co-management was supposed to avoid any opposition between employers and employees, prevent class conflict, and nip in the bud any tendency toward protest. On the level of the enterprise, the autonomy of the free, joyful co-worker was supposed to do away with divisions in society (rich/poor, right/left, worker/boss, etc.) and ensure the productive community's unity of will, affect, and action.

Germany's past, the obsession of all the nationalists, and among them, the Nazis, had been nothing but division among tribes (*Stämme*), and then among states, because of the political fragmentation (*Kleinstaaterei*) resulting from the Treaties of Westphalia (1648), and finally between social classes, because of German industrial modernization, and especially the teachings of Marxism's false prophets. The Nazi leaders had sought, at any price, to escape this fate and exorcize division: political unity (a single party in 1933, a single, central political power with the abolition of the *Länder* in 1934) had to prevail, along with cultural and social unity, through unity of race.

Escaping division remained the obsession of the hierarchs of the Federal Republic of Germany who, in addition to their rejection of the political division between the FRG and the GDR (the latter being officially recognized only in 1973), absolutely sought to prevent social division. In a "social" market economy with co-management based on dialogue between "social partners" on almost equal terms, the management Höhn envisaged made a decisive contribution to the edifice—the cornerstone, at the foundation, at the level of the enterprise itself.

Thanks to Ludwig Erhard, the minister who conceived of harmony and collaboration at the national level, and to Reinhard Höhn, who designed it at the business level, Germany's present was characterized entirely by formal freedom, productive efficiency, and a high growth rate. Its future, which was already outlined, would be that of a model, a beacon of the free world confronting the neighboring GDR and the Soviet world and acting as an economic and political flagship product, and even, when the time came, as a strategic bridgehead.

However, seeing "subordinates" as "co-workers" and, better yet, as beings endowed with thought and autonomy, certainly could not be taken for granted in the German economic universe, which cultivated a sense of the caricatural hierarchy inspired by what was most rigid in the army—despite Scharnhorst. The writer Heinrich Mann, Thomas's brother, provided a good example of this in *The Loyal Subject*, a famous satirical novel published in 1913. It narrates the mediocre, conformist, and authoritarian life of a chemist, reserve military officer, loyal subject of the Emperor Wilhelm II, and militaristic CEO. This world, made still more stringent by the war economy prevailing between 1936 and 1945, was ruled by the old military maxim that advised people to leave reflection to the horses, because they have the biggest heads. Höhn seemed to be a pioneer and a visionary, if not a revolutionary. The conversion of the former SS-man to the principles of individualism and autonomy was clearly apparent: between what Höhn advocated and wrote from 1933 to 1945 and what he taught starting in 1956, there was no break, but rather an impressive continuity in ideas.

During the twelve years of Nazi domination in Germany, a regime hostile to democracy claimed, through the voice of its jurists and theoreticians, to be the realization of "Germanic" liberty. After 1945, one of its intellectuals conceived of a non-authoritarian kind of management—an apparent paradox for a former SS-man, but apparent only for someone who wanted to break with the absolutist state, or indeed with any kind of state, and bring about the advent of freedom of initiative for agents and agencies.

This freedom was, however, a contradictory injunction: in the form of management Höhn imagined, people were free to obey, free to realize the objectives determined by the *Führung*. The only freedom resided in the choice of means, never in the choice of ends. Höhn was, in fact, anything but a libertarian or anarchist: the thousands of enterprises (2,440 between

1956 and 1969) that sent him their managers were fully aware of that.

The functioning of the organization claimed to be non-authoritarian, but it remained thoroughly hierarchical, because the fundamental relationship was still between boss and agent. The boss, contrary to the practices in force up to that point, did not prescribe the action in the most precise details of its execution. He limited himself to issuing "directives" in terms of "objectives." His role was to order (a result, for example), and then to observe, supervise, and evaluate:

> Superiors make no decisions in the domain of their co-workers. They limit themselves to their managerial duties, which consist essentially in defining objectives, providing information, coordinating, and controlling [. . .]. The hierarchy that was based on the fact of giving orders becomes a hierarchy of responsibility [. . .]. The delegation of responsibility therefore does not mean a dissolution of the hierarchy, but rather a change in its function and significance.[127]

The agent, for his part, was recruited on the basis of a job description (*Stellenbeschreibung*), a creation to which Höhn gave prestige, and which specified the employee's duties, mission, and capabilities. Between the boss and the employee there was now a "relationship of collaboration" (*Mitarbeiterverhältnis*), also known as "delegation of responsibility" (*Delegation von Verantwortung*).

Reading Höhn, one might think his method has only merits: cooperation, subsidiarity, freedom:

> Decisions are no longer made by a single individual or a group of individuals at the head of the enterprise, but, in each case, by co-workers at the level that characterizes them. The co-workers are no longer directed by precise orders

issued by their superior. On the contrary, they have at their disposition a well-defined field of action in which they are free to act and make decisions autonomously, thanks to the precise jurisdictions allotted to them.[128]

But the responsibility for commanding, and henceforth, for supervising and evaluating, was assigned to the boss. The responsibility for acting and succeeding was incumbent upon the employee, and this responsibility was all the greater because he was free to choose the avenues and the means best adapted to the execution of his mission. The compensation, in terms of responsibility, was clearly decreed by Höhn, who wrote, as if heaving a sigh of relief:

> Responsibility is therefore no longer concentrated solely and uniquely on management. Part of this responsibility is in fact transferred [. . .] to the level that is entrusted with taking action.[129]

Paradoxes are thus added to contradictions. A first apparent paradox: a former SS-man imagining a non-authoritarian management model. A second paradox: the contradictory injunction involved in the freedom to obey. This accumulation of contradictions seems to constitute a very real perversion, in the most classic sense of the term: the Bad Harzburg method, like related methods of management by objectives, is based on a fundamental lie, and causes the employee or subordinate to veer from a promised freedom toward a certain alienation that comforts the *Führung*, the "direction," which no longer bears alone the responsibility for any potential or actual failure.

The consequence of these contradictions and this perversion is anything but merely theoretical: never thinking about ends, being confined solely to calculating means, is constitutive of an alienation on the job whose psychosocial symptoms are well-known: anxiety, exhaustion, "burn-out," and the form of inner resignation that is now called "bore-out," a kind of "inner resignation" on which Reinhard Höhn, who at the age of 79 was still keeping abreast of new developments, wrote two pioneering books in 1983.[130]

Despite these flaws and these risks, Dr. Höhn's solution seemed to be the panacea and universal response to the problems of organization that were arising everywhere in both the private and the public sectors. In 1969, the Akademie added "special seminars" (*Sonderseminare*) for managers who were public officials (at the levels of the state, the *Länder*, and the communes) and wanted to be trained in "modern methods of management."[131] To provide this training, the academy's press began a series of studies dealing specifically with administrative management, and in 1970 Höhn published a 448-page volume devoted to this topic. No doubt tired of publishing and reprinting manuals and practical guides full of schemas and bullet points, here Höhn donned the toga of the *Universitätsprofessor* and lawyer specializing in public law that he never ceased to be, enjoying the opportunity to resituate the question of public management in a long-term history of administration and power. In his view, what had been true about the army and the economy was true about the civil service: "The administration's management style proceeded straight out of the world of absolutism that founded the modern state."[132] Therefore, "the administration [had to be] reformed" so that it could be adapted, in its management and its organization, to the demands of industrial society as well as to a modern economy that had to be able to see the administration as a partner implementing the same principles."[133]

There had once been a time when nascent enterprises took inspiration from the structure of public administration to create their own flow charts. That time was over, and the relationship between the model and the disciple had been reversed: "The administration is [. . .] no longer a model for the economy;"[134] on the contrary, he wrote, it had to "follow a transformation in which the economy has preceded it."[135] There was nothing preventing "modern methods of management being transposed to the administration."[136] In fact, this transposition was a necessity—an economic necessity accompanied and reinforced by the logic of the time, that of the democratic, parliamentary Constitution that governed the FRG. Must we wait for a parliamentary initiative, a reform law? Must we "wait or begin?"[137] Höhn advocated action and a *fait accompli*. As a good disciple—admittedly, a renegade one—of Carl Schmitt, Höhn wanted authority to put an end to the relationship of authority, just as Schmitt wanted the exception to re-establish normality:

> No director of an administration needs to wait for a law handed down from on high. On the contrary, he can do by himself what he deems necessary. [. . .] He can decide that these new principles of management are now obligatory for all members of his department. That would be the last act of authority that would put an end to authoritarian management.[138]

These bosses, full of initiative and courage, could be sure that they would not be "marginal; they [could] be confident that their acts correspond[ed] to the trend of their time and that they [were] acting in conformity with the spirit of progress."[139]

Thus, the growing lack of difference between administration and enterprise, between public sector and private sector, was seen as progress. The same principles of organization and the same criteria of evaluation must be applied to the two orders. A few years in advance of practices in Britain, America, and Scandinavia, Höhn, who foresaw in the 1930s the decay of the state and the development of agencies, made himself the precursor, if not the prophet, of the "New Public Management" that has become almost a state religion in Western countries, beginning with the Germany of Chancellor Helmut Kohl in the early 1980s.

Public administration was thus brought into conformity with the principles of the private economy. The same went for the army: the hierarchy of the Bundeswehr had long admired the works of Reinhard Höhn, whose influence on modern conceptions of command is widely acknowledged. The former SS-man and follower of the Third Reich turned out to be a *spiritus rector* of the "citizen in uniform" in democratic Germany. Moreover, officers and non-commissioned officers were sent to Bad Harzburg to imbibe his words and principles at the source.

T he revelation of his status in the SS, along with deeper research into Reinhard Höhn's past, provoked a scandal and marked the beginning of very real difficulties for him and for his academy.

The blow came from the left, in this case from *Vorwärts,* the historic newspaper published by the Social Democratic Party (Sozialdemokratische Partei, SPD). However, the SPD had its own secrets: one of its heroes, the "super minister" of the economy, Karl Schiller, who was also a professor and held a doctorate, had a proven Nazi past as a member of the NSDAP and the SA—and, furthermore, he left the SPD to join the Free Democratic Party (FDP) and ended up on the extreme right. On December 9, 1971, Professor Schiller's past still discreetly under wraps, *Vorwärts* lingered on that of Professor Höhn with an article entitled "The Forge of the Elites. Where bosses learn to command. At the headquarters in Bad Harzburg, ex-general Höhn teaches against democracy." The author wrote an unflinching indictment of the academy and its founder, using facts publicly known and published since the 1950s and subsequently collected in 1965 in a work entitled *The Brown Book. War Criminals and Nazi Criminals holding office in the FRG. State, economy, army administration, judicial system, sciences,*[140] published in East Berlin by the GDR. Two devastating pages are devoted to Höhn, presented as an "SS officer and crown attorney for Himmler." In 1966–67, a series of 21 articles on the SS in *Der Spiegel* quoted Höhn seven times. In 1966, the professor-manager was also questioned by the special court in Ludwigsburg entrusted with tracking down and indicting Nazi war criminals. Höhn was suspected of having participated, as a department head (*Amtschef*) of the SD, in a meeting held in Berlin on September 11, 1939 that discussed the killing of 60,000 members of the Polish elites. Höhn vigorously defended himself. Owing to lack of proof, the special court had to abandon its legal proceedings against him after a few hearings.

The repercussions of the 1971 article were immense. In 1969, the social-liberal coalition led by the SPD and Chancellor Willy Brandt, a former member of the anti-Nazi resistance, had put an end to the Grand Coalition led by the former Nazi Kurt Georg Kiesinger, who had been slapped during a CDU meeting by Beate Klarsfeld. Now the time had come to settle scores with a number of former Nazis under pressure from university students, a fringe group of which engaged in direct action against the "fascism" of their parents and their Republic; this Red Army Faction was, moreover, to assassinate Höhn's former student Hanns Martin Schleyer in 1977. An open letter signed by famous writers, including Siegfried Lenz, Erich Kästner, and Günther Wallraf, was addressed to the Minister of Defense, Helmut Schmidt. A few months later, in March, 1972, the minister made a decision: the Bundeswehr's cooperation with the Bad Harzburg Akademie would cease.[141]

In addition to the difficulties Professor Höhn encountered when his past in the SS caught up with him, there were also the theoretical and practical challenges mounted against the Bad Harzburg model; in the 1970s and 1980s, it was increasingly seen as ponderous and unwieldly, because it was too precise and too bureaucratic. Höhn's various works did not in fact limit themselves to setting forth the principle of management by delegation of responsibility and to singing the praises of *Auftragstaktik* applied to economic production. They also explained, using a multitude of case studies, how *Auftragstaktik* should be implemented. The managers who came to be trained in his school had to understand and assimilate approximately 315 rules governing the application of the method, starting with the creation of very precise job descriptions for employees, as well as the many norms that regulated the relations and communication between employees and bosses, which were themselves organized in staffs.

In 1972, the weekly newspaper *Die Zeit* devoted a long article to the new methods of management that were competing with and threatening the "delegation of responsibility" model.[142] They came from Switzerland, and, especially, from the United States.

In the 1980s, it became clear, in universities and various training institutes, that the Bad Harzburg method was losing ground to the "management by objectives" method emanating from America. The Austrian Peter Drucker had been developing it since the 1950s, at the same time that Höhn was thinking about his own method. Management by objectives seemed to be a "lite" version—more flexible and, in a word, more liberal—of Höhn's approach: it seemed the professor and former senior official of the SS had not fully succeeded in ridding himself of a Prussian administrative ethos dependent (like management by objectives) on supervision, and replete with rules, index cards, papers, and stamps of all kinds.

In 1979, the German periodical *Managermagazin* unceremoniously declared Höhn and his model dead: following his precepts meant remaining in "the Stone Age." On the occasion of its seventieth anniversary in 1974, the monthly published a very critical portrait of Höhn, the interview not sparing him questions about the problems, indeed the dead-ends, of his method, while at the same time praising his virtues as a teacher, concluding that the weaknesses of the management model were largely compensated for by their creator's showmanship in lectures. Nonetheless, "management by delegation" was, in fact, "the most German of all the models of management: serious and bureaucratic." In 1983, this periodical, respected in the world of business, maintained its view that the former SS man, now 79 years old, was an "old-timer."[143]

In 1989, the Bad Harzburg Academy, which had suffered considerably from the attacks on Höhn's reputation, went into receivership. Its activities were separated: the Cognos company, managed by Daniel Pinnow, one of Höhn's former students, took over the seminars under the brand Die Akademie, while the distance-learning operation became the Bad Harzburg Wirtschaftsakademie (Business Academy). The "Akademie" now enrolled 10,000 students a year, as compared with 35,000 in Höhn's heyday. The school and its website continued to praise the former Nazi jurist and SS general as a great management thinker and incomparable creator of the institution.

In the 1990s, Höhn gave up teaching and limited himself to overseeing the republication of some of his works. His last publication dates from 1995, when he was 91 years old. He died in the year 2000, a little before the biblical age of 96. The obituaries in the major German newspapers saluted the brilliant manager, the talented teacher, and the indefatigable scientific researcher.

It is revealing that the method's problems resulted from its creator's personality, from the character of a past that was too overtly Nazi and had become disturbing, and not from the incompatibility between economic and political culture. The FRG's economic and political culture had welcomed with fervor Bad Harzburg's management model, which was perfectly compatible with it: ordoliberalism claimed to be a supervised liberty, while the social market economy sought to integrate the masses through participation and co-management, in order to avoid class conflict and slipping into "Bolshevism." Höhn never abandoned his basic conceptual framework, which was simultaneously a principle and an ideal—that of the community, preferably a closed community. It was, in fact, after 1949, a community built on careers, mindsets, and culture that "reconstructed" the foundations of economic production, the state, and the army. Postwar managers had all prepared for the fray under the Third Reich, and many of them had emerged from the SD and SS. The personal transition—that of careers—and the conceptual transition—that of ideas—was generally not too difficult: "Germanic freedom" became freedom, period, the "armament effort" was transformed into reconstruction, and the "Judeo-Bolshevik" enemy became merely the Soviet counterpart. Reinhard Höhn was, both before and after 1945, a man of his time.

It is only really today that the question arises of how a society, unique and unprecedented in human history, could tolerate economic practices that are so manifestly antagonistic to its most fundamental principles. "Fear-based management" and the almost absolute alienation of individuals, reduced to a mere "labor factor," to a simple "human resource," or just another kind of "productive capital," have been accepted in our societies on the rationale, or the pretext, that they are demanded by "globalization" and its competitive reality. That, Höhn had not foreseen, even though in the 1940s he had dreamed of a unified economic area in the Germanic *Großraum*. But in this context as well, his method could still be used.

In recent years, Reinhard Höhn and the Bad Harzburg method have in fact received public attention once again. In 2012, a manager working for the Aldi chain, a monument of German consumer society since the 1950s and the true inventor of "discount stores," published a book on his painful experience as the manager of one of the firm's distribution centers. In *Aldi, Simply Cheap: A Former Manager Tells All*,[144] Andreas Straub describes an oppressive culture of monitoring and constant harassment. From the outset, Aldi has proudly adhered to the Bad Harzburg method of management, as is made clear in its handbook for managers. The rubric M4, entitled "Managing Co-workers," explains:

> The sector manager will seek to develop discussion with the team as a whole by applying the Harzburg model. This model of management is characterized by the principle of delegation, that is, the transfer of tasks and responsibilities to a co-worker, the latter accepting critical supervision and monitoring by the hierarchical superior. The hierarchical superior sets for each co-worker individual objectives and time frames for carrying them out. Their role is to recognize and nurture the abilities of their co-workers and to practice constructive criticism centred on dialogue.[145]

This paragraph, which is distinguished neither by its literary quality nor by even the most elementary grasp of language, is nonetheless eloquent: the obligatory passage on "constructive criticism" and the culture of "dialogue" leaves no doubt as to what has been taken from the Bad Harzburg method, or rather, as to how the latter is concretely put into practice. The essential point is the setting of "objectives," the prescription of "time frames" for carrying them out, and the exercise of "monitoring." That is exactly what Andreas Straub describes, as the German weekly *Der Spiegel* also did when it published, on April 30, 2012, a feature on this "company drunk on monitoring."[146] In an interview with the magazine, the author of the book declares that "the system lives on total monitoring and fear."[147] Any means of ensuring the "maximization of profit" seems to be acceptable: the monitoring of tasks and the time it takes to carry them out is constant, and includes filming employees. Because this procedure is illegal, Aldi prefers to send "monitors" into its stores to make "test purchases" that seek to evaluate the performance of the cashiers. Every shortcoming, every failure—there is always one—is recorded, and serves to justify dismissal when the time comes. To "throw someone out," the entire monitoring record is made available. In the course of a tense interview, a totally constructed "pressure situation is created." "Two or three people accuse the employee of failures" in order to make them crack and accept a mutually-agreed-upon resignation contract (*Aufhebungsvertrag*) that allows the company to avoid making severance payments and thus significantly reduces the cost of termination. The strategy of tension reaches its peak in this intense scenario but it is also a regular feature of employment, according to Straub and *Der Spiegel*'s journalists: "The harassment and massive pressure are constant."

In Aldi-Süd, where Straub worked, "works councils" did not exist; they were "absolutely forbidden [. . .]. Management was clear: it would not allow anyone to meddle in its affairs." Thus, there was no one to monitor the monitors.

I n 1954, Reinhard Höhn, employed by the German Soci ety for Political Economy (Deutsche Volkswirtschaftliche Gesellschaft) think tank, was preparing to set up his management school in Bad Harzburg. At the same time, Maurice Papon, former secretary-general of the prefecture of La Gironde during the German occupation of France, then prefect of Corsica and the department of Constantinois in Algeria, published an essay on management entitled *L'Ère des responsables*.[148] Writing in a flat, descriptive manner, Papon, who at that time was the secretary-general of the Paris police, delivers with irritating solemnity his decision-maker's lessons for the benefit of the public sector and private enterprise. No doubt he was putting down a marker for a new career outside the administration, for a cozy transition to a better job that came later, in 1967. After a very satisfactory performance as the head of the Paris police, notably during his flawless repression of the demonstrations on October 17, 1961 against "the events" in Algeria, Maurice Papon became president of Sud Aviation (later to become Aérospatiale, a state-owned aerospace manufacturer). He then embarked upon a career in politics, as deputy to the National Assembly, and then as prime minister Raymond Barre's budget minister from 1978 to 1981, at the end of Valéry Giscard d'Estaing's presidency.

Management, which used to be called "*organisation*" in French, is a way of thinking about structures of labor, the assignment of tasks, and the definition of skills and responsibilities. As such, it was able to blossom in contexts of liberal capitalism, as it did in France with Fayol or in the United States with Taylor from the end of the nineteenth century on, just as it did in the Russia/USSR of the Bolshevik Revolution or in Nazi Germany. It is a neutral instrument that can be used for good or bad ends (like science, one might say, but is science ever really a neutral instrument?), to ensure the proper functioning of a children's hospital or that of a factory making tanks. That is probably true, but too simple.

Management as a full-fledged discipline, in theory and in practice, resulting in specialized schools ("of commerce," of "business," or simply of "management"), consulting firms, and dedicated positions, is also an indication or symptom of a peculiar social organization. The "era of accountability" or "the bosses' century"[149] and the time of "processes" prevailed in the second half of the nineteenth century. This was the period of large systems of production, of the "management" of the industrial era's masses and the fragmentation of labor into tasks and specialized functions.

It then transpired that what was prevalent in stores and workshops, and even in manufacturing—intuition, interpersonal relations, a form of improvisation—was no longer valid for large units of production and huge cohorts of workers. The era of mass production was that of the bosses, to be sure, but it was also that of engineering consultants,[150] and then of consultants in organization, direction, and management. In a largely "disenchanted" world, one where matter is to be transformed and nature is to be dominated, the purely immanent horizon is summed up in production and profit or, more precisely, in the augmentation of the former and the optimization of the latter. This holds, it is true, everywhere: from the Renault factories in Billancourt and the Citroën factories in Javel to the gigantic factory in Detroit where the Ford Model T was produced; from Stalin's USSR of the Five-Year Plans to Nazi Germany.

The latter offers an interesting vantage point from which to think about management and our modernity. Nazi Germany, which was in the grip of an ideology in action, was the paradoxical site of a "reactionary modernity"[151] that put all the resources of scientific, technological, and organizational modernity in the service of a project that was partly archaic in its return to origins and zoological warfare. From our point of view, the effort to seek consent, or even to elicit support, in a country we usually consider to have been, from 1933 on, an immense, open-air prison, a vast concentration camp—is paradoxical. While part of the population was indeed incarcerated, this was not true for the immense majority of people, provided that they were considered to be of the "right race," kept quiet and were not political trouble-makers. Far from being a simple alliance between the microphone (propaganda) and the truncheon (repression) behind barbed wire and under observation from watchtowers, Nazi Germany was a complex organization in which the authorities sought to purchase consent by contentment and engaged in almost constant negotiation—at least tacit—with its people, except resisters, until the fall of 1944, at the height of war and disaster, when violence broke out against those who were lukewarm or reluctant.

This political reality, more participative than repressive, had an ideological aim—to bring into being, against the society of class struggle, the community of the "race comrades" (*Volksgenossen*), a Germany united in its battle for life, disencumbered of the simultaneously harmful and false ideas of liberal individualism or Marxism. It also had an economic *raison d'être*: to establish itself in the arena of nations, to assert itself within the zoo-enclosure of history, to survive the competition of other peoples and races, and also to make up for its slowness to act, Germany had to produce in quantity and dominate broadly. To produce, it had to create a military force and armaments that would allow it to resume the war where it had left off, to Germany's detriment, in 1918–19. To dominate, it had to conquer a *Lebensraum*, that is, literally, a "biotope," for its population that would also be a hinterland for its industry and provide raw materials (wood from Poland, metals from Russia) and energy (oil from the Caucasus, food from Ukraine). The Reich, Hitler complained, had been poorly endowed by nature with a meager territory relative to its legitimate ambitions and the excellence of the Germanic race.

German production also required laborers and employees who were convinced of the necessity of their tasks and enthusiastic about their work. Nazi *Menschenführung* (leadership of people) had to replace the rigid and authoritarian *Verwaltung* (administration) of earlier times. The "workforce," "capital," or "human material" (*Menschenmaterial*) could be fully exploited and made profitable only if it was free and happy, autonomous and rich in initiatives—or at least had the illusion of being all that.

At the intersection of the ideological, the political, and the economic, Nazi *Menschenführung*, the idea of management, was one of the main expressions of the characteristic of the Third Reich that historians have constantly emphasized for the past thirty years, in both cultural history[152] and social history:[153] this regime was participative, because it sought to produce consensus.

The regime that seems to us the most repressive ever (and it was, I repeat, for the hundreds of thousands of Germans who were its victims for "political" or "racial" reasons) thus encouraged and financed works and reflections on a non-authoritative mode of organization. The model—according to Reinhard Höhn, who never gave up on it—was quintessentially German, that is, Prussian: in the shock of the defeat in 1806, the reformers of the Prussian army elaborated mission-type tactics (*Auftragstaktik*) so that non-commissioned officers and soldiers might have a taste of the intoxicating autonomy felt by the French citizen-soldiers in the armies of the Revolution and the Empire. Orders had to be vague and general, and be limited to setting objectives ("take that hill before nightfall," for example): the person who received an order was free to choose the best avenue, means, and method to carry it out. This limited autonomy also entailed a greater responsibility: success was expected, and failure betrayed the personal failure of the person who did not succeed in accomplishing the mission. Autonomy was also superficial: the subordinate was free to choose the means, but certainly not to define the end—to set the objective.

For the jurist and SS general Reinhard Höhn, who was passionately interested in questions of organization and military history, the reform of *Auftragstaktik* constituted the *nec plus ultra* of freedom of action. After 1945, and particularly after opening his academy in Bad Harzburg in 1956, Höhn transposed this military and administrative model to the private economy and reinvented himself as a thinker specializing in the management of services and industry. In dozens of works and in thousands of seminars, he transformed *Auftragstaktik* into "management by delegation," which was supposed to be anti-authoritarian and thus certifiably democratic and *bundesrepublikanisch*. Whereas the Bundeswehr adopted the principle of the soldier's *innere Führung* ("autonomous conduct"), in part on his advice, the German economic miracle was nourished by the "delegation of responsibility" for which more than 200,000 managers were trained by Höhn and his teams between 1956 and 1972, and almost 500,000 afterward, up until his death in the year 2000.

Höhn's method of management, which was hierarchical without being authoritarian, offered "co-workers" the enjoyment of a structured freedom that left them free to succeed by achieving, in the best possible way, a goal they themselves had not defined. In perfect continuity with what he had advocated before 1945, Höhn imagined a participative organization.

Before 1945, the worker and the employee were companions (*Betriebsgenossen*) of the leader (*Führer*), and no longer his class enemy. After 1949, in the FRG, it was a time for generalized participation, for the co-management sought by Konrad Adenauer and Ludwig Erhard to avoid class war and any risk of communist temptation. In this context, the Bad Harzburg doctrine served as an official catechism in business enterprises, armies, and then administrations, a sort of factory and state religion in harmony, thanks to the autonomy and freedom it seemed to guarantee, with the new truths of a liberal democracy and economy.

Reinhard Höhn was a former senior official in the SD and the SS who had risen to the rank of general by the end of the war. That was well known to all those in the army and private industry who sent their managers for training in Bad Harzburg, where the faculty included two other former senior officials in the SS, Justus Beyer and Franz Alfred Six, who had begun new careers as professors of marketing, as well as a Nazi physician fanatical about eugenics and racism, Professor Kötschau, who now showered exhausted managers with advice about diet and ergonomics. Times had to change, a generation had to pass and the Social Democrats had to come to power for Höhn's luck to turn after 1971. The scandalous publicity regarding his past did a disservice to his school, while his method of management now seemed too rigid, too closed to the new sirens of teamwork and "team-building"—which did not prevent Höhn from continuing to publish until 1995 (when he was 91 years old) and to be saluted, when he died in May, 2000, as a great thinker of contemporary management by a press whose obituaries were initially unanimous, from the right (*FAZ*) to the left (*Süddeutsche Zeitung*). Such was the destiny of this ideologist and radical technician who succeeded so well in re-inventing himself and pursuing his second career. This itinerary says a great deal about Germany and Europe during the Cold War: the networks of solidarity among former SS-men were very active in promoting the enterprise and guaranteeing the prosperity of Professor Dr. and SS-*Oberführer* Reinhard Höhn.

It also has almost the value of a parable for reading and understanding the world in which we live. Höhn was sagacious and clever enough to renounce what motivated him and what he affirmed before 1945 concerning "sub-humans," foreigners, and Jews. In his postwar writings, we no longer find any trace of anti-Semitism or racism, which were so fundamental for the Nazi worldview. However, one thing remains in this jurist who loved military history: the idea that life is a war and that it is appropriate to seek the methods and formulas for an efficient, high-performance organization in the work of those who reflected on the German army. A hard worker, indefatigable teacher, feverishly productive writer, and networker who was constantly active, Höhn retained from Nazism the idea that, in the struggle for life as in economic war, one had to perform well and encourage performance. He was an unapologetic Darwinist who was accordingly at ease in the world of the "economic miracle" between 1950 and 1970: high growth, productivity, and competition were all notions that the Nazis had brought to a point of frenzy in their insatiable race toward production and domination. To be profitable/successful/productive (*leistungsfähig*) and to assert oneself (*sich durchsetzen*) in a competitive world (*Wettbewerb*), to win (*siegen*) in the battle for life (*Lebenskampf*)—after 1945, Höhn adopted all these expressions typical of Nazi thought, and we still use them all too often today. The Nazis didn't invent them—they were inherited from the West's military, economic, and eugenicist Social Darwinism of the period between 1850 and 1930—but the Nazis incarnated and illustrated them in a way that ought to lead us to reflect on who we are, what we think, and what we do.

Must we, as machines among other machines, make our bodies hard as steel (*stählern*) in fitness centers? Do we have to "battle" and be "fighters"? Must we "manage" our lives, our loves, and our emotions, and be successful in economic war? These ideas lead to the reification of the self, of the other, and of the world—the generalized transformation of every existence, every being, into "objects" and "factors" (of production), to the point of exhaustion and devastation.

The example of Reinhard Höhn—admittedly extreme—shows this: "management" and its reign are not neutral, but rather integral to an age of the masses, of production and destruction that had its heyday in Europe and the United States between 1890 and 1970. A first blow was struck against it by the oil crises of 1973 and 1979, and a second blow, which occurred after 2000, with the growing realization that our thermo-industrial civilization, our way of life and production, are already threatening our life on Earth itself.

The disconnect with regard to the nature and reality of production, of a person's realization through work, and the growing evaporation of the meaning and pleasure that each individual can find in his or her salaried occupation, leaves to our contemporaries only this curious abstraction of the "structure" and the problems it creates. Traditional production, that of the farmer and the craftsman, collided with the concrete, real difficulties of land and resources. In the age of the tertiary sector and exploding virtuality, the organization of labor seems to have become the sole reality: getting a "job" and then being evaluated and evaluating others often becomes the only goal of a completely self-referential "career" that has no purpose other than itself, unless it is simply perceived, by the employee themself as a "bullshit job"[154] that has to be done to pay one's bills, pass the time, and comply with a certain imperative of social normality. In this world, management is king, and the most painful problems one encounters (physical and psychological problems that sometimes lead to suicide) are the very ones that it seems to create.

The Bad Harzburg model was not worse than the others; on the contrary. It was promising, and, in any case, full of future prospects that were less authoritarian. It turned out to be perverse, as perverse as a (former) Nazi celebrating freedom. The observation of contemporary managerial reality hardly elicits more optimism: present-day social and judicial actuality, from petty bosses to human tragedies, from the France Telecom case to Amazon warehouses, offers a very dark picture of productive organization. Is that inevitable? Is everything in managerial thought and reality problematic, harmful, or perverse? Without bringing up the Fall and the hasty departure from the original paradise, or an uncontrollable anthropological inevitability, we can conclude that the problem resides in the almost blind faith with which a hypostatized "management" is referred to in the world of work, where it has become the law and the prophets. The law, because the work of the theorization of labor relations, which is often banal and not very interesting, or is even intellectually impoverished, is constantly cited as recourse or as an excuse. The prophets, because "management" has become a metonymy: it designates not only a theoretical activity and a body of principles, but also those who apply it, as well as a kind of totem or idol, a calf that is made not of gold but of lead.

More deeply, we can conclude that the problem resides in the bond of subordination inherent in the labor contract, which stipulates that an agent X must carry out a task defined by a superior Y—no matter how he does so, and no matter what the characteristics of the relationship between X and Y (authoritarian or liberal, harassing or trusting). The question of the autonomy that can be left to Y is the one that preoccupies all those who reflect on organization and what distinguishes all managerial theories—or modes of management—from the strict, quasi-military subordination of someone like Fayol to the more recent practices of "freed" enterprise, passing by way of all the nuances (or all the excesses) of constraint and performance: authoritarian management, management by objectives, by stress, by fear, or, in reaction, "slow management," or management that is benevolent or humanistic.

The problem of autonomy, if not of liberty, is basically the one that has arisen for philosophers and thinkers concerned with the city since at least the seventeenth century: how to give up the state of nature and its dangers without abdicating too much of one's natural freedom in the society thus created? This question, which is foundational for contractualist thinking, social contract theories, and contemporary *societies*, is resolved by theorists of the *community* like Reinhard Höhn and his fellow jurists under the Third Reich. The community is the natural and spontaneous union of free men, free by nature because of the very fact that they obey, because in obeying the *Führer*, they are obeying only themselves, that is, only the purest and healthiest instinct of the German race. What is true at the level of the Reich is also true at the level of the *Betrieb*, of the business enterprise, which is driven by a "community" of leaders and comrades (*Genossen*) or co-workers (*Mitarbeiter*). For a self-respecting manager, the question of freedom is foolish and pointless: one is free by definition, by the simple fact that one is participating in the community, whether the latter be a *Gemeinschaft* or a team.

The question of freedom, in and despite the group, profoundly nourished the reflection and debate on political society in the seventeenth and eighteenth centuries—without ceasing to be asked, moreover—before coming also to concern economic society and the business enterprise, which became, in the nineteenth century, a mass organization and reality in the production sectors of both goods and services. In the age of the masses, the status of the salaried employee was reduced to a payroll unit, and organizational mammoths appeared whose internal structure became a "science"—that of management, to be precise. Political thinkers, who were paying attention to this

economic development, replied very early on that salvation resided in rejection—the rejection of hierarchy, of authority, the
refusal of constraint and subordination—in short, in anarchy,
in the strictest sense of the term (the refusal of the power of
constraint). Their response ushered in a new political society,
without economic societies or business enterprises, unless they
were very small. The ideal, as per Rousseau early on, turned out
to be the independent worker—the clockmaker or stone-cutter,
the free producer or artist lauded by Proudhon and cherished
by his compatriot Courbet, who shared his ideas. These authors
and these ideas never ceased to inspire alternative practices,
ranging from egalitarian cooperatives to neo-rural re-training
programs, by way of managers tired of their alienation who re-
discovered a craft activity in which they could finally be independent. An un-archaic Arcadia, freed from subordination and
management, but not a paradise for all that. The reality of work,
of the effort to provide, of a certain anxiety regarding the result,
remains, but without the alienation. How sweet it is to work for
oneself, say people who are happily remodeling a house or re-
viving a vegetable garden. Is that naïve and irresponsible solip-
sism? Maybe not, as is shown by the success of a social economy
based on solidarity—and the sharing of the vegetables from the
aforementioned garden: it is possible to work for oneself and
still be useful to others. This is the antithesis of the structures,
ideals, and world of Reinhard Höhn, to whom we may prefer
Hegel: human labor is non-alienated labor, which allows the
mind to *re*alize and know itself through the production of a
thing (*res*) that expresses and resembles it—whether a pastry or
a plant cutting, a book or a manufactured object—and not the
activity that reifies the individual, turns one into an object—a
"human resource," "labor factor," or "payroll unit"—doomed
to "benchmarking," to an evaluation interview and the inevitable PowerPoint meeting.

Training women and men to obey by considering them

simple production factors, and devastating the Earth, conceived as a simple object, go hand in hand. By encouraging the destruction of nature and the exploitation of "life force" to an unprecedented degree, the Nazis appear to be the deformed and revelatory image of a modernity gone mad—served by illusions (the "final victory" or the "resumption of growth") and by lies ("freedom," "autonomy") whose clever creators were management thinkers like Reinhard Höhn.

However, Höhn's personal destiny shows that ideas have their time and their authors have their era. Höhn suffered from the revelations about his past and from the criticisms directed against his managerial model—internal criticisms, for which other models paved the way.

The times can also change under the influence of more general and more urgent circumstances: the way we see ourselves, others, and the world—steeped in "management" and "struggle" by a few decades of highly productivist economics and by well-targeted distractions (from the quiz show *The Weakest Link* to reality television's competitive games)—may change because of the completely unrealistic character of our economic organization and our "values."

Perhaps our children will consider all this as foreign and distant as we now consider the young SS-man and the old professor in Bad Harzburg ruminating on the Reich's defeat and trying to make it acceptable by turning his country into an economic giant.

APPENDICES

SELECTED BIBLIOGRAPHY

Agamben, Giorgio, *Homo Sacer: Sovereign Power and Bare Life*, translated by Daniel Heller-Roazen. Stanford, Calif.: Stanford University Press, 1998.

Agamben, Giorgio, *Means Without End: Notes on Politics*, translated by Vincenzo Binetti and Cesare Cesarino. Minneapolis: University of Minnesota Press, 2000.

Bajohr, Frank and Wildt, Michael (eds.), *Volksgemeinschaft. Neue Forschungen zur Gesellschaft des Nationalsozialismus*, Frankfurt: Fischer Verlag, 2009.

Bauman, Zygmunt, *Modernity and the Holocaust,* Cambridge, UK: Polity Press, 1989.

Boltanski, Luc and Chiapello Ève, *The New Spirit of Capitalism*, translated by Gregory Elliott. London; New York: Verso, 2005.

Braunbuch. Kriegs- und Naziverbrecher in der Bundesrepublik. Staal, Wirtschaft, Armee, Verwaltung, Justiz, Wissenschaft, Berlin: Nationalrat der nationalen Front des Demokratischen Deutschland und Dokumentationszentrum der Staatlichen Archivverwaltung der DDR, 1965.

Car, Ronald, "Community of neighbors vs. society of merchants. The genesis of Reinhard Höhn's state theory," *Politics, Religion and Ideology*, vol. 16, no. 1, 2015, pp. 1–22.

Chamayou, Grégoire, *The Ungovernable Society: A Genealogy of Authoritarian Liberalism*, translated by Andrew Brown. Medford: Polity Press, 2021.

Chapoutot, Johann, *The Law of Blood: Thinking and Acting as a Nazi*, translated by Miranda Richmond Mouillot. Cambridge, Massachusetts: The Belknap Press of Harvard University Press, 2018.

Chapoutot, Johann, *La Révolution culturelle nazie*, Paris: Gallimard, coll. Bibliothèque des Histoires, 2017.

Cohen, Yves, *Le Siècle des chefs. Une histoire transnationale du commandement et de l'autorité, 1890-1940,* Paris: Éditions Amsterdam, 2013.

Crawford, Matthew, *Shop Class as Soulcraft. An Inquiry Into the Value of Work*, London-New York: The Penguin Press, 2009.

Dreier, Horst, Pauly, Walter et al., *Die deutsche Staatsrechtslehre in der Zeit des Nationalsozialismus*, Berlin: De Gruyter, 2000.

Dujarier, Marie-Anne, *Le Management désincarné. Enquête sur les nouveaux cadres du travail*, Paris: La Découverte, 2015.

Frei, Norbert (ed.), *Karrieren im Zwielicht. Hitlers Eliten nach 1945*, Frankfurt-New York: Campus Verlag, 2002.

Gall, Lothar and Pohl, Manfred (eds.), *Unternehmen im Nationalsozialismus*, Munich: Beck Verlag, 1998.

Gauléjac, Vincent de, *La Société malade de la gestion. Idéologie gestionnaire, pouvoir managérial et harcèlement social*, Paris: Éditions du Seuil, 2005.

Grünbacher, Armin, "The Americanisation that never was? The first decade of the Baden-Badener Unternehmergespräche, 1954-64 and top management training in 1950s Germany," *Business History*, vol. 54, no. 2, April 2012, pp. 245–262.

Grünbacher, Armin, *West German Industrialists and the Making of an Economic Miracle. A History of Mentality and Recovery*, London: Bloomsbury, 2017.

Hachmeister, Lutz, *Der Gegnerforscher. Die Karriere des SS-Führers Franz Alfred Six*, Munich: Beck Verlag, 1998.

Hachmeister, Lutz, "Die Rolle des SD-Personals in der Nachkriegszeit. Zur nationalsozialistischen Durchdringung der

Bundesrepublik," in Michael Wildt (ed.), *Nachrichtendienst, politische Elite und Mordeinheit. Der Sicherheitsdienst des Reichsführers SS*, Hamburg: Hamburger Edition, 2016, pp. 347–369.

Hachmeister, Lutz, *Schleyer. Eine deutsche Geschichte*, Munich: Beck Verlag, 2004.

Henry, Odile, *Les Guérisseurs de l'économie. Sociogenèse du métier de consultant, 1900-1944*, Paris: CNRS éditions, 2012.

Herbert, Ulrich, *Best: biographische Studien über Radikalismus, Weltanschauung und Vernunft, 1903-1989*, Bonn: J.H.W. Dietz, 1996.

Herbert, Ulrich, "Generation der Sachlichkeit," in Frank Bajohr (ed.), *Zivilisation und Barbarei. Die widersprüchlichen Potentiale der Moderne. Detlev Peukert zum Gedenken*, Hamburg: Christians, 1991, pp. 115–144.

Herf, Jeffrey, *Reactionary Modernism. Technology, Culture, and Politics in Weimar and the Third Reich,* Cambridge, UK: Cambridge University Press, 1984.

Höhn, Reinhard, *Revolution, Heer, Kriegsbild,* Darmstadt: Wittich, 1944.

Ingrao, Christian, *Believe and Destroy: Intellectuals in the SS War Machine*, translated by Andrew Brown. Cambridge, UK; Malden, MA: Polity, 2013.

Jouanjan, Olivier, *Justifier l'injustifiable. L'ordre du discours juridique nazi*, Paris: PUF, 2016.

Jouanjan, Olivier, "Reinhard Höhn, juriste, SS, manager," in Marc-Olivier Baruch (ed.), *Faire des choix? Les fonctionnaires dans l'Europe des dictatures, 1933-1948*, Paris: La Documentation française, 2014, pp. 99–125.

Kaienburg, Hermann, *Die Wirtschaft der SS*, Berlin: Metropol Verlag, 2003.

Klee, Ernst, "Kötschau, Karl, Prof. Dr.," in *Das Personenlexikon zum Dritten Reich. Wer war was vor und nach 1945*, Frankfurt: Fischer Taschenbuch Verlag, 2nd. ed., 2007, p. 327.

Konitzer, Werner and Palme, David (eds.), *"Arbeit," "Volk," "Gemeinschaft." Ethik und Ethiken im Nationalsozialismus*, Frankfurt-New York: Campus Verlag, 2016.

Legendre, Pierre, Dominium mundi. *L'empire du management*, Paris: Mille et une nuits / Fayard, 2007.

Lindner, Stephan, *Inside IG Farben: Hoechst during the Third Reich*, translated by Helen Schoop. Cambridge, New York: Cambridge University Press, 2008.

Linhart, Danièle, *La Comédie humaine du travail. De la déshumanisation taylorienne à la sur-humanisation managériale*, Toulouse: Érès, 2015.

Linhart, Danièle, "La subordination au travail: entre consentement et contrainte?," in Patrick Faugeras (ed.), *L'Intime Désaccord. Entre contrainte et consentement*, Toulouse: Érès, 2017, pp. 223–240.

Mantel, Peter, *Betriebswirtschaftslehre und Nationalsozialismus. Eine institutionen- und personengeschichtliche Studie*, Wiesbaden: Gabler Verlag, 2009.

Meinel, Florian, *Der Jurist in der industriellen Gesellschaft. Ernst Fortshoff und seine Zeit*, Berlin: Akademie Verlag, 2011.

Müller, Alexander, *Reinhard Höhn. Ein Leben zwischen Kontinuität und Neubeginn*, Berlin: Be. Bra Wissenschaft Verlag, 2019.

Rebentisch, Dieter, *Führerstaat und Verwaltung im Zweiten Weltkrieg. Verfassungsentwicklung und Verwaltungspolitik 1939-1945*, Stuttgart: Steiner, 1989.

Rebentisch, Dieter and Teppe, Karl (eds.), *Verwaltung contra Menschenführung im Staat Hitlers. Studien zum politisch-administrativen System*, Göttingen: Vandenhoeck & Ruprecht, 1986.

Reichel, Peter, *Der schöne Schein des Dritten Reiches. Faszination und Gewalt des Faschismus*, Munich: Carl Hanser Verlag, 1991.

Reuber, Christian, *Der lange Weg an die Spitze. Karrieren*

von Führungskräften deutscher Grossunternehmen im 20. Jahrhundert, Frankfurt: Campus Verlag, 2012.

Rüthers, Bernd, "Reinhard Höhn, Carl Schmitt und andere – Geschichten und Legenden aus der NS-Zeit," *Neue Juristische Wochenschrift*, 39, 2000, pp. 2866–2871.

Saldern, Adelheid von, "Das 'Harzburger Modell.' Ein Ordnungssystem für bundesrepublikanische Unternehmen, 1960-1975," in Thomas Etzemüller (ed.), *Die Ordnung der Moderne. Social Engineering im 20. Jahrhundert*, Bielefeld: Transcript Verlag, 2009, pp. 303–329.

Schmid, Daniel C., "'Quo vadis, Homo harzburgensis?' Aufstieg und Niedergang des 'Harzburger Modells,'" *Zeitschrift für Unternehmensgeschichte*, vol. 59, no. 1, 2014, pp. 73–98.

Schroeder, Klaus-Peter, *"Eine Universität für Juristen und von Juristen." Die Heidelberger juristische Fakultät im 19. und 20. Jahrhundert*, Tübingen: Mohr Siebeck, 2010.

Schulte, Jan Erik, *Zwangsarbeit und Vernichtung. Das Wirtschaftsimperium der SS. Oswald Pohl und das SS Wirtschafts-Verwaltungshauptamt 1933-1945*, Paderborn: Schöningh, 2001.

Smelser, Ronald and Syring, Enrico (eds.), *Die SS: Elite unter dem Totenkopf. 30 Lebensläufe*, Paderborn: Schöningh, 2000.

Smelser, Ronald, Syring, Enrico and Zitelmann, Rainer (eds.), *Die braune Elite II. 21 weitere biographische Skizzen*, Darmstadt, Wissenschaftliche Buchgesellschaft, 1993.

Stiegler, Barbara, *"Il faut s'adapter." Sur un nouvel impératif politique*, Paris: Gallimard, coll. NRF Essais, 2019.

Stolleis, Michael, *A History of Public Law in Germany, 1914-1945*, translated by Thomas Dunlap. Oxford; New York: Oxford University Press, 2004.

Supiot, Alain, *Le Travail n'est pas une marchandise. Contenu et sens du travail au XXIe siècle*, Paris: Éditions du Collège de France, 2019.

Tooze, Adam, *The Wages of Destruction. The Making and*

Breaking of the Nazi Economy, London: Penguin Books, 2007.

Wildt, Michael, "Der Fall Reinhard Höhn. Vom Reichssicherheitshauptamt zur Harzburger Akademie," in Alexander Gallus and Axel Schildt (eds.), *Rückblickend in die Zukunft. Politische Öffentlichkeit und intellektuelle Positionen in Deutschland um 1950 und um 1930*, Göttingen: Wallstein Verlag, 2011, pp. 254–274.

Wildt, Michael, *An Uncompromising Generation: The Nazi Leadership of the Reich Security Main Office*, translated by Tom Lampert. Madison, Wis.: University of Wisconsin Press, 2009.

Notes

Prologue

[1] Christian Ingrao, *Les Chasseurs noirs. La Brigade Dirlewanger*, Paris: Perrin, 2006.

[2] Nicolas Patin, *Krüger, un bourreau ordinaire*, Paris: Fayard, 2017.

[3] Robert Gerwarth, *Hitler's Hangman. The Life of Heydrich*, New Haven: Yale University Press, 2011.

[4] Joachim Lehmann, "Herbert Backe, Technokrat und Agrarideologe," in Ronald Smelser, Enrico Syring and Rainer Zitelmann (eds.), *Die braune Elite II. 21 weitere biographische Skizzen*, Darmstadt: Wissenschaftliche Buchgesellschaft, 1993, pp. 1–12; Herbert Backe, *Deutscher Bauer, erwache! Die Agrarkrise, ihre Ursachen und Folgerungen*, Munich: Boepple, Nationalsozialistische Agrarfragen, 1931, p. 31.

[5] Herbert Backe, "12 Gebote für das Verhalten der Deutschen im Osten und die Behandlung der Russen," 1 June 1941, p. 3.

[6] Cf. Gesine Gerhard, "Food and genocide. Nazi agrarian politics in the occupied territories of the Soviet Union," *Contemporary European History*, vol. 18, no. 1, February 2009, pp. 45–65.

[7] Cf. in particular Götz Aly, *"Endlösung". Völkerverschiebung und der Mord an den europäischen Juden*, Frankfurt: Fischer Verlag, 1995.

[8] Michael Allen, *The Business of Genocide. The SS, Slave Labor, and the Concentration Camps*, Chapel Hill: University of North Carolina Press, 2002, and id., "Oswald Pohl, Chef der SS-Wirtschaftsunternehmen," in Ronald Smelser and Enrico Syring (eds.), *Die SS: Elite unter dem Totenkopf. 30 Lebensläufe,* Paderborn: Schöningh, 2000, pp. 394–407.

[9] Rainer Fröbe, "Hans Kammler, Technokrat der Vernichtung," in Ronald Smelser and Enrico Syring (eds.), *Die SS*, pp. 305–319.

[10] Cf. in particular Magnus Brechtken, *Albert Speer. Eine deutsche Karriere*, Munich: Siedler Verlag, 2017, and Martin Kitchen, *Speer. Hitler's Architect*, New Haven: Yale University Press, 2015.

[11] Cf. Marie-Anne Dujarier, *Le Management désincarné. Enquête sur les nouveaux cadres du travail*, Paris: La Découverte, 2015.

[12] A "resource," even if it is "human" can be quantified, counted, and thus "managed." The older term "personnel" referred a little more to the "person."

Chapter 1
Conceiving the Administration of the Great Reich

[13] Waldemar Ernst, "Erlebnis und Gestaltung deutscher Grossraumverwaltung," *Reich, Volksordnung, Lebensraum. Zeitschrift für völkische Verfassung und Verwaltung*, vol. V, 1943, p. 269.

[14] Ibid., p. 270.

[15] Gerhard Rolfs, "Erfassung der Unterlagen für eine planmässige Verwaltungsführung," *Reich, Volksordnung*, pp. 285–295. (All English versions are the translator's.)

[16] Wilhelm Stuckart, "Zentralgewalt, Dezentralisation und Verwaltungseinheit," in Wilhelm Stuckart, Werner Best, et al., *Festgabe für Heinrich Himmler*, Darmstadt: Wittich, 1941, pp. 1–32, p. 2 for the preceding quotation.

[17] Ibid., p. 1.

[18] Ibid., p. 5.

[19] Ibid., p. 7 and p. 31.

[20] Ibid., p. 4.

[21] Ibid.

[22] Ibid., p. 5.

[23] Ibid.

[24] Ibid., p. 6.

[25] Walter Labs, "Die Verwaltung der besetzten Ostgebiete," *Reich,*

Volksordnung, Lebensraum. Zeitschrift für völkische Verfassung und Verwaltung, vol. V, 1943, p. 137.

[26] "Erlaß des Führers und Reichskanzlers über die Vereinfachung der Verwaltung vom 28. August 1939," *Reichsgesetzblatt*, no. 153, 30 August 1939, pp. 1535–1537.

[27] Wilhelm Stuckart, "Die Neuordnung der Kontinente und die Zusammenarbeit auf dem Gebiete der Verwaltung," *Reich, Volksordnung, Lebensraum. Zeitschrift für völkische Verfassung und Verwaltung*, vol. I, 1941, p. 27.

[28] Wilhelm Stuckart, "Zentralgewalt, Dezentralisation und Verwaltungseinheit," in Wilhelm Stuckart, Werner Best et al., *Festgabe für Heinrich Himmler*, p. 13.

[29] Ibid.

[30] Ulrich Herbert, *Best: biographische Studien über Radikalismus, Weltanschauung und Vernunft, 1903–1989*, Bonn: J.H.W. Dietz, 1996.

[31] Werner Best, "Grundfragen einer deutschen Grossraum-Verwaltung," in Wilhelm Stuckart, Werner Best et al., *Festgabe für Heinrich Himmler*, p. 33.

[32] Ibid., p. 37.

[33] Ibid., pp. 38–39.

[34] Ibid., p. 40.

CHAPTER 2

MUST THE STATE BE ABOLISHED?

[35] Cf. Johann Chapoutot, *La Révolution culturelle nazie*, Paris: Gallimard, coll. Bibliothèque des Histoires, 2017, chapter 2: "La dénaturation du droit nordique. Droit germanique et réception du droit 'romain,'" pp. 53–72.

[36] *Robert Koch, Bekämpfer des Todes* (Hans Steinhoff), Tobis, 113 min, 1939, BA-FA 187456.

[37] *Carl Peters* (1941), 117 min., BA-FA 10102. Based on a screenplay by Ernst von Salomon.

[38] Reinhard Höhn, *Die Wandlung im staatsrechtlichen Denken*, Hamburg: Hanseatische Verlagsanstalt, 1934.

[39] Ibid., p. 35.

[40] Ibid., p. 36.

[41] Ibid.

[42] Reinhard Höhn, "Volk, Staat und Recht," in Reinhard Höhn, Theodor Maunz and Ernst Swoboda, *Grundfragen der Rechtsauffassung*, Munich: Duncker & Humblot, 1938, pp. 1–27.

[43] Ibid., p. 26.

[44] Reinhard Höhn, *Verwaltung heute. Autoritäre Führung oder modernes Management?*, Bad Harzburg: Verlag für Wissenschaft, Wirtschaft und Technik, 1970, p. 1.

[45] Ibid., p. 2.

CHAPTER 3
"GERMAN LIBERTY"

[46] Heinrich Himmler, in Werner Best, Hans Frank, Heinrich Himmler and Reinhard Höhn, *Grundfragen der deutschen Polizei. Bericht über die konstituierende Sitzung des Ausschusses für Polizeirecht der Akademie für deutsches Recht am 11. Oktober 1936*, Hamburg: Hanseatische Verlagsanstalt, Arbeitsberichte der Akademie für deutsches Recht, 1936, p. 12.

[47] Reinhard Höhn, *Die Wandlung im staatsrechtlichen Denken*, p. 9.

[48] Ibid., p. 9.

[49] Ibid., p. 12.

[50] Ibid., p. 10 and p. 34.

[51] Ibid., p. 36.

[52] Ibid., p. 42.

[53] Ibid., p. 36.

[54] Ibid., p. 34.

[55] *Der Herrscher* (Veit Harlan), UFA, 1937, 99 min, BA-FA 10274.

[56] Cf. Dieter Rebentisch and Karl Teppe (eds.), *Verwaltung contra Menschenführung im Staat Hitlers. Studien zum politischadministrativen System*, Göttingen: Vandenhoeck & Ruprecht, 1986, and Dieter

Rebentisch, *Führerstaat und Verwaltung im Zweiten Weltkrieg. Verfassungsentwicklung und Verwaltungspolitik 1939–1945*, Stuttgart: Steiner, 1989.

CHAPTER 4
THE NAZI MANAGEMENT OF HUMAN RESOURCES

[57] Ludwig Ferdinand Clauss, *Rasse und Seele. Eine Einführung in den Sinn der leiblichen Gestalt*, Munich: Lehmann Verlag, 1926. Cf. also Ludwig Ferdinand Clauss, *Die nordische Seele – Eine Einführung in die Rassenseelenkunde*, Munich: Lehmann Verlag, 1933.

[58] Adam Tooze, *The Wages of Destruction. The Making and Breaking of the Nazi Economy,* London: Penguin Books, 2007.

[59] Götz Aly, *Hitlers Volksstaat. Raub, Rassenkrieg und nationaler Sozialismus*, Frankfurt: Fischer Verlag, 2005.

[60] Johann Chapoutot, "*Suum cuique* et 'justice naturelle' sous le IIIe Reich," in Christine Mengès-Le Pape (ed.), *La Justice entre théologie et droit*, Toulouse: Presses de l'Université Toulouse I Capitole, 2016, pp. 633–640.

CHAPTER 5
FROM THE SS TO MANAGEMENT: REINHARD HÖHN'S AKADEMIE FÜR
FÜHRUNGSKRÄFTE

[61] Michael Wildt, *Generation des Unbedingten. Das Führungskorps des Reichssicherheitshauptamtes,* Hamburg: Hamburger Edition, 2002, and Christian Ingrao, *Croire et détruire. Les intellectuels dans la machine de guerre SS*, Paris: Fayard, 2010.

[62] A biography of Reinhard Höhn comparable to the one Ulrich Herbert wrote about Werner Best has long been lacking. Two historians, Michael Wildt and Lutz Hachmeister, have taken an interest in him, as has the jurist Olivier Jouanjan: Olivier Jouanjan, "Reinhard Höhn, juriste, SS, manager," in Marc-Olivier Baruch (ed.), *Faire des choix ? Les fonctionnaires dans l'Europe des dictatures, 1933–1948*, Paris: La Documentation française, 2014, pp. 99–125 ; Lutz Hachmeister, "Die

Rolle des SD-Personals in der Nachkriegszeit. Zur nationalsozialistischen Durchdringung der Bundesrepublik," in Michael Wildt (ed.), *Nachrichtendienst, politische Elite und Mordeinheit. Der Sicherheitsdienst des Reichsführers SS*, Hamburg: Hamburger Edition, 2016, pp. 347–369; Michael Wildt, "Der Fall Reinhard Höhn. Vom Reichssicherheitshauptamt zur Harzburger Akademie," in Alexander Gallus and Axel Schildt (eds.), *Rückblickend in die Zukunft. Politische Öffentlichkeit und intellektuelle Positionen in Deutschland um 1950 und um 1930*, Göttingen: Wallstein Verlag, 2011, pp. 254–274. It is only recently, in the summer of 2019, that an initial biography of Höhn, derived from a dissertation defended at the Technische Universität in Chemnitz, has appeared in Germany: Alexander Müller, *Reinhard Höhn: ein Leben zwischen Kontinuität und Neubeginn*, Berlin: Be. Bra Wissenschaft Verlag, 2019.

[63] Reinhard Höhn, *Die Stellung des Strafrichters in den Gesetzen der französischen Revolutionszeit (1791–1810)*, Berlin: De Gruyter, 1929.

[64] Reinhard Höhn, *Der individualistische Staatsbegriff und die juristische Staatsperson*, Berlin: Heymann, 1935.

[65] Lutz Hachmeister, *Schleyer, eine deutsche Geschichte*, Munich: Beck Verlag, 2004.

[66] Carl Schmitt (ed.), *Das Judentum in der Rechtswissenschaft. Ansprachen, Vorträge und Ergebnisse der Tagung der Reichsgruppe Hochschullehrer des NSRB am 3. und 4. Oktober 1936—1 —Die deutsche Rechtswissenschaft im Kampf gegen den jüdischen Geist*, Berlin: Deutscher Rechtsverlag, 1936.

[67] Michael Wildt, "Der Fall Reinhard Höhn. Vom Reichssicherheitshauptamt zur Harzburger Akademie," in Alexander Gallus and Axel Schildt (eds.), *Rückblickend in die Zukunft*, p. 259.

[68] Ibid., p. 266.

[69] Lutz Hachmeister, "Die Rolle des SD-Personals in der Nachkriegszeit. Zur nationalsozialistischen Durchdringung der Bundesrepublik," in Michael Wildt (ed.), *Nachrichtendienst, politische Elite und Mordeinheit*, p. 349.

[70] Ibid., p. 351.

[71] Lutz Hachmeister, *Der Gegnerforscher. Die Karriere des SS Führers Franz Alfred Six*, Munich: Beck Verlag, 1998.

[72] Franz-Alfred Six, *Marketing in der Investitionsgüterindustrie*.

Durchleuchtung, Planung, Erschliessung, Bad Harzburg: Verlag für Wissenschaft, Wirtschaft und Technik, 1971.

CHAPTER 6
THE ART OF (ECONOMIC) WAR

[73] Reinhard Höhn, *Scharnhorsts Vermächtnis*, Bonn: Athenäum Verlag, 1952, 2nd edition, Frankfurt, Bernard & Graefe Verlag für Wehrwesen, 1972.

[74] Ibid., p. 68 et *passim*.

[75] Ibid., p. 75.

[76] Ibid.

[77] Ibid.

[78] Ibid., p. 76.

[79] Ibid.

[80] Ibid.

[81] Ibid.

[82] Ibid., p. 68.

[83] Ibid., p. 65.

[84] Ibid.

[85] Ibid., p. 66.

[86] Ibid., p. 67.

[87] Ibid., p. 13.

[88] Ibid., p. 16.

[89] Ibid., p. 14 ff.

[90] Ibid., p. 15.

[91] Ibid., p. 16.

[92] Ibid., p. 15.

[93] Ibid., p. 16.

[94] Ibid., p. 102.

[95] Ibid.

[96] Ibid.

[97] Ibid., p. 103.

[98] Ibid., p. 107.

[99] Ibid., p. 105.

[100] Ibid., p. 107 and 117 ff.

[101] Ibid., p. 117.

[102] Ibid.

[103] Ibid., p. 110.

[104] Ibid., p. 107.

[105] Ibid., p. 136.

[106] Ibid., p. 118.

[107] Ibid., p. 119.

[108] Ibid., p. 121.

[109] Ibid., p. 134.

[110] Ibid.

[111] Ibid., p. 137.

[112] Ibid., p. 138.

[113] Ibid., p. 139 and 141.

[114] Ibid., p. 140.

[115] Ibid., p. 141.

CHAPTER 7
THE BAD HARZBURG METHOD:
THE FREEDOM TO OBEY, THE OBLIGATION TO SUCCEED

[116] Norbert Frei (ed.), *Karrieren im Zwielicht. Hitlers Eliten nach 1945*, Frankfurt-New York: Campus Verlag, 2002.

[117] Nikolas Lelle, "'Firm im Führen.' Das 'Harzburger Modell' und eine (Nachkriegs-) Geschichte deutscher Arbeit," in Werner Konitzer and David Palme (eds.), *"Arbeit," "Volk," "Gemeinschaft." Ethik und Ethiken im Nationalsozialismus*, Frankfurt-New York: Campus Verlag, 2016.

[118] Reinhard Höhn, *Das tägliche Brot des Managements. Orientierungshilfen zur erfolgreichen Führung*, Bad Harzburg: Verlag für Wissenschaft, Wirtschaft und Technik, 1978.

[119] Reinhard Höhn, *Die Sekretärin und der Chef. Die Sekretärin in der Führungsordnung eines modernen Unternehmens*, Bad Harzburg: Verlag für Wissenschaft, Wirtschaft und Technik, 1965.

[120] Reinhard Höhn, *Die Geschäftsleitung der GmbH. Organisation, Führung und Verantwortung*, Köln: Schmidt, 1987.

[121] Reinhard Höhn, *Das Unternehmen in der Krise. Krisenmanagement und Krisenstab*, Bad Harzburg: Verlag für Wissenschaft, Wirtschaft und Technik, 1974.

[122] Reinhard Höhn, *Die Technik der geistigen Arbeit. Bewältigung der Routine, Steigerung der Kreativität*, Bad Harzburg: Verlag für Wissenschaft, Wirtschaft und Technik, 1979.

[123] Reinhard Höhn, *Das tägliche Brot des Managements*, p. 47.

[124] Ibid.

[125] Reinhard Höhn, *Reich, Grossraum, Grossmacht*, Darmstadt: Wittich, 1942, p. 85.

[126] Ibid.

[127] Reinhard Höhn, *Verwaltung heute. Autoritäre Führung oder modernes Management?*, *Vorwort* [Foreword], p. VIII.

[128] Reinhard Höhn, *Das Harzburger Modell in der Praxis*, Bad Harzburg: Verlag für Wissenschaft, Wirtschaft und Technik, 1970, p. 6.

[129] Ibid.

[130] Reinhard Höhn and Gisela Böhme, *Die Sekretärin und die innere Kündigung im Unternehmen. Ihr Verhalten im Spannungsfeld zwischen Chef und Mitarbeitern*, Bad Harzburg: Verlag für Wissenschaft, Wirtschaft und Technik, 1983, and Reinhard Höhn, *Die innere Kündigung im Unternehmen. Ursachen, Folgen, Gegenmassnahmen*, Bad Harzburg: Verlag für Wissenschaft, Wirtschaft und Technik, 1983.

[131] Reinhard Höhn, *Verwaltung heute*, p. VII.

[132] Ibid., p. VII.

[133] Ibid., p. X.

[134] Ibid.

[135] Ibid., p. XI.

[136] Ibid.

[137] Ibid., p. 406.

[138] Ibid., p. 408.

[139] Ibid., p. 411.

CHAPTER 8
THE TWILIGHT OF A GOD

[140] *Braunbuch. Kriegs- und Naziverbrecher in der Bundesrepublik. Staat, Wirtschaft, Armee, Verwaltung, Justiz, Wissenschaft,* Berlin: Nationalrat der nationalen Front des Demokratischen Deutschland und Dokumentationszentrum der Staatlichen Archivverwaltung der DDR, 1965.

[141] Michael Wildt, "Der Fall Reinhard Höhn. Vom Reichssicherheitshauptamt zur Harzburger Akademie," in Alexander Gallus and Axel Schildt (eds.), *Rückblickend in die Zukunft*, pp. 267–268.

[142] Rosemarie Fiedler-Winter, "Management nach Schweizer Art," *Die Zeit*, 28 July 1972.

[143] Michael Wildt, "Der Fall Reinhard Höhn," pp. 268–269.

[144] Andreas Straub, *Aldi, einfach billig. Ein ehemaliger Manager packt aus*, Reinbek: Rowohlt Taschenbuch Verlag, 2012.

[145] Aldi, *Manuel Responsable Secteur*, no place or date, Rubric M4 (not paginated).

[146] "Konzern im Kontrollrausch," *Der Spiegel*, 30 April 2012.

[147] "Das System lebt von totaler Kontrolle und Angst," *Der Spiegel*, 2 May 2012.

EPILOGUE

[148] Maurice Papon, *L'Ère des responsables. Essai sur une méthodologie de synthèse à l'usage des chefs dans la libre entreprise et dans l'État*, Tunis: La Rapide, 1954.

[149] Yves Cohen, *Le Siècle des chefs. Une histoire transnationale du commandement et de l'autorité, 1890–1940*, Paris: Éditions Amsterdam, 2013.

[150] Odile Henry, *Les Guérisseurs de l'économie. Sociogenèse du métier de consultant, 1900–1944*, Paris: CNRS éditions, 2012.

[151] Jeffrey Herf, *Reactionary Modernism. Technology, Culture, and Politics in Weimar and the Third Reich,* Cambridge, UK: Cambridge University Press, 1984.

[152] See the pioneering study by Peter Reichel on the Third Reich as a spectacle and as an enterprise of seduction: *Der schöne Schein des Dritten Reiches. Faszination und Gewalt des Faschismus*, Munich: Carl Hanser Verlag, 1991.

[153] Frank Bajohr and Michael Wildt (eds.), *Volksgemeinschaft. Neue Forschungen zur Gesellschaft des Nationalsozialismus,* Frankfurt: Fischer Verlag, 2009.

[154] David Graeber, *Bullshit Jobs*, New York: Simon & Schuster, 2018.

Index of Names